# EDITOR

FIONA SAMPSO

*P*oetry Review, fair, fat and a hundred years old, is full of Christmas cheer this December, thanks to Carol Ann Duffy and Stephen Raw's panels from the Laureate's *Manchester Carols*. Elsewhere, this is an issue brimful of personalities. A remarkable collection of poems about people – from elegy to epithalamium – is followed by a Centrefold entirely given over to poet-on-poet portraits. Anne Stevenson discusses her peer Anne Sexton, John Kinsella writes on Michael Donaghy, and Sean O'Brien surveys Don Paterson's work. The section closes with Wendy Cope's encomium for Jonathan Barker, and a chapter from Gwyneth Lewis's *Hospital Odyssey*, in which her alter ego undertakes that terrifying journey which is accompanying a loved one through treatment. As well as the usual range of reviews, we've some wonderful writerly second thoughts from Peter Blegvad, and Ruth O'Callaghan's account of literary *entente* in Mongolia.

2009 opened with the death of *PR*'s former editor, the poet Mick Imlah, and as the year draws to an end the death of John Smith, who edited the magazine from 1962-6, has been announced. Smith, who sometimes used the pseudonym C. Busby, published several collections with, among others, the Hogarth Press and Hutchinson. His work also included a verse-play and anthologies.[1]

But 2009 has also been the year in which the Society and its magazine celebrated their centenaries (both, interestingly, underwent a name-change in their very earliest years) by looking both back and forwards. For the *Review* that has meant discovering, though the process of compiling its centenary anthology, just what an important part this oldest and most widely read of British poetry magazines has played in the formation of both canon and poetry culture. It's proved possible to trace not only the literary fashions of each decade but vertical threads of influence – such as a lineage of women poets, the recurring reinvention of Scottishness, or the importance of critics like Stewart Brown and (poet-critic) Archie Markham to BME writing in Britain[2] – and this in turn leads to the humbling understanding that what the *Review* does now matters not only to the literary present but for the literary future too. Only the best will do – for you the reader and for future readers too! An exciting thought for the New Year.

---

1 I am indebted to Alan Brownjohn for this information.
2 Royalties from the sale of *A Century of Poetry Review* go to the foundation of the *Review*'s E.A. Markham prize for BME critical writing.

*from* The Manchester Carols
*Carol Ann Duffy and Stephen Raw*

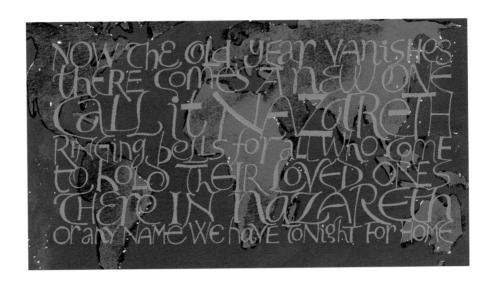

YOU BEAR THE CHRISTMAS CHILD AND HE WILL LIVE AND DIE WITHIN YOUR ARMS. SORROW AND JOY RESIDE IN YOU YOU BEAR THE CHRISTMAS CHILD

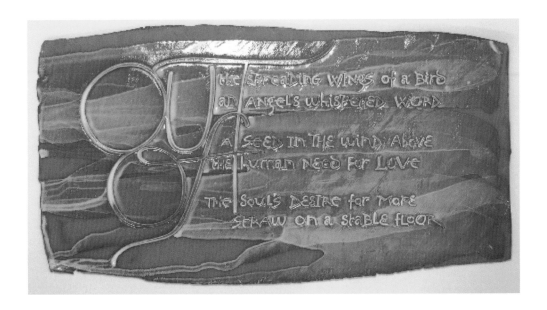

# Contents

## Volume 99:4 Winter 2009

# Full Length Portraits

# Critical Views

# Album

# POEMS

But what is a book without love?
— *Lyubomir Levchev*

*David Harsent*
## Five Poems

## Blood Heat

Full length under a wide white sky in a place like this, or a place
you think you remember, or wherever it is she happens to turn her face

to the sun, eyes open a moment, then the flare and crush
of red behind the lids and you at her side to watch the sudden blush

that prickles her skin, the first fine hint of burn, as you get
the tip of your tongue to her cheek for the salt-lick of her sweat.

## Blood Relative

His footsteps in yours, the moment of waking that same
redeye view of the world, his dottle deep

in your lung, his kiss your gift to give: the sudden sharp
dip of his head, the bloodbead on a lover's lip,

his arrival in the room your moment of fame,
his easy laugh, his clever guess, his word to the wise the sum

of all you are, all you could ever be, and your other name,
given in passion, in trust, is nothing more than a slip

of the tongue, and no-one but yourself to blame
for the hand-in-hand, the cheek-to-cheek, the side-by-side as you sleep.

# Bloodstain

*Drench of the death-bed that drains to the floorboards and hangs*
*like a sweat of dew on the ceiling below...* and where you found

that graceless image is for you alone to know, but it brings
with it a tang of salt, and a dry day by the sea then comes to mind:

raw sky and a cutting wind that left the man half-blind
from a scrap of something blown in from the other shore,

the tear of blood he caught up with his tongue, the nip of fear
you felt as he put his head in your hands while you took

the mote on the tip of your finger, his shudder-sigh, his empty look
no different now to then, perhaps, except for the dew of the sea on his cheek.


# Blood Alley

Your childhood token, a sickle of red in the glass, albino eye,
eye of the night-lamped hare; a perfect lob would break the circle...

Now hold it close to the light and every fibril
seems to shred, as heart-blood hangs in water, that same dark dye,

shade of the dress she wore when you had your first full taste
of the pulp of her lip and the spittle off her tongue, the cost

to you being more than you had to give, which is why
the circle must break again and the dream unpick and the child be lost.


*Blood Alley:* The name given to a large marble – a tolley – clear glass except for a twist of
red at its heart.

# Bloodvein

*(i.m.)*

Soft on a leaf, last of the garden exotica, found only at dusk and pale
as the face in the sick-bed except for that long line
going wing-tip to wing-tip, heartstring, nerve-track, a thread you
might pull

were it not for the way she turns and settles her head, the long vein
in her throat showing lilac by lamplight... The shadows that peel
from her fingers as they spread must be part of some long scene

of doubt and decay where all of this plays out: the fractured pearl
of the creature's eye, the journey from leaf to lamp that has long been
written in, like your word to her, like hers to you as she palms the
bitter pill.

*Bloodvein*: The moth of this name is a pale cream colour save for a line of red that goes from
wing-tip to wing-tip.

*Linda Gregerson*
*from* The Life Of St Peter

*(Brancacci Chapel, Florence)*


## The Death Of Ananias
*(Acts 5:1-10)*

There must have been something with-
           held as if
you know the story you'll
      know has been said about me.

I saw what we all saw: goats and cattle,
         grain,
an ancient and three newer family
      houses and finally

the second-best vineyard for miles around
        converted
into silver and simply
      laid on the ground at their feet.

And namely the one called Peter: how
        is it
that one among equals will seem
      to have harnessed the moon

and stars. I understood the next
        part, how the
logic went: we hadn't been
      savages all our lives, we'd helped

the poor before. But this was something
                    else, was like
the dizzying vista above the gorge:
          you think you've been quite

happy, your loved ones are waiting to
                welcome you
home and you can taste the broken rocks
          below through all your broken

teeth, you know the terror won't be
                over until
you've thrown your one allotted life
          away. And so

I stepped back, just a little, from the
                edge.
What kind of reckoning after all requires
          this all-or-nothing? Hadn't I

torn the lovely acres from my heart?
                Which he
esteemed as so much filth. The least
          that would keep the cold off, that's

all I'd intended to put aside. You
                see?
And cold came up to seize me.

## The Tribute Money

Then, said my Master, *are the children*
       *free.* Which you might think
              would tell us what to do

       but we had caught the scent
of parable. So hook, so fish, the
              money in its mouth,

              the mucus and blood
       on the money. I paid the collector
as I'd been told and part

was the lesson and part was speaking
       truth to power and still
              there's part left over.

       From whom, he said, do the kings
of the earth extract their tribute?
              Shining in its mouth as

              shines the golden hair
       you see to my left in the picture. From
the stranger, we said. But he

my Master loved said nothing, nothing
       but beauty was ever required
              of him. *Then are*

       *the children free.* Now look,
I'm not immune to this, I like
              to work the likeness out:

for *pieces of money* read
*gifts of the earth*, for *hook*
read *yours for the asking*. But as to

the one with golden hair, read what?
That some shall leap while others
crawl? That even

the best of love is partial?
The fish that flashed a thousand
colours, though you throw

him back, will drown.
Which makes me think
the gills in their air-scorched frenzy must

extract some tribute too.

*Sigitas Parulskis*
# Underground Garages

I love underground garages, cool, crammed
with twilight, parking
slots you dive into, as into Pluto's realm, and later
come back into light, afraid to look in the rearview
mirror in case you've left something vital
there, under the ground
mythology here is offside –
to put it simply, a green sign shines out 'Spaces Free'
in the evening twilight,
which means that there
under the ground, spaces are free

there's something very human about a garage, people
arrive in cars,
abandon them and go somewhere, shoved by their worries
and joys, and return later,
sit in their motion machines and transport themselves
completely elsewhere, to the city's edge, its suburbs, to another
city, to another world, however they manage it

one day each and every one of us will leave
our motion
machines, our bodies, and transport ourselves
there, where spaces are, where
spaces are never lacking,
where it doesn't smell of petrol, of fresh snow, of rain,
of sperm, of tears, of treason, where there are no
windscreen wipers, no warning signs,
where no one speeds because all motorways,
even the fastest, bring to mind a falling
shadow breathing, and more than that, nothing –
if the essence of this word
could surpass itself

Translated by Matthew Sweeney

*Sean O'Brien*
# Going Below At Railway Fields

Having no choice but to finish the sentence
You learn to read over again.

The railway fields, their asphalt paths,
The bonfire smell of dusk, the dusk
Deeper each second yet barely begun.
It is nowhere you know. It is home.

Your sandshoes leak and then go black.
The grass itself is largely asphalt,
The same way the railway embankment
Is several parts clinker and several parts
Old flattened coins from a city of childhood
You're too tired now to imagine in detail.

*

The smell of ash, like schools and hospitals,
Bodily clinker laid down as
A brown-purple edge to the field,
In the lee of the papery heeled-over fences

That might have been sheds
With a smoke and a paper, here
To get the benefit of dusk, the blue workers
Stealing an inch but reliably finding

They can't get the wood, though the trees –
Which are aspen and birches
And pause like the corps de ballet in the long yellow grass
At the foot of the siding – are plentiful still.

*

Going below, where the dark leads, the sun is put
Back in the suitcase with straps and a label:

*Malaya Singapore Port Said Akratiri –*
Feel the heat off that, eh?
                              This landscape
Is death, but the fact
Is not uppermost, not while the train comes
Trailing skirts of steam, pausing and pulling away
With a press-roll of iron on iron,
Not with a viaduct left to walk under
Still ringing with transport and sunset, not
With the heat of the day in the pavement,
The soles of your feet, not back in the kitchen,
The afterlight still there to read by.

*Robin Robertson*
# Easter, Liguria

Another day watching the ocean move
under the sun; pines, wisteria, lemon trees.
I darken this paradise like a sudden wind:
olive leaves, blown on their backs, silver
to razor-wire; cameras click in the wall.

Everyone is going home, and I realise
I have no idea what that means.
I listen to the shrieking of the gulls
and try to remember. How long ago
did I notice that the light was wrong,
that something inside me was broken?
Standing here, feeling nothing at all.
How long have I been leaving?
I don't know.

# Landfall

The fishboxes
of Fraserburgh, Aberdeen,
Peterhead, the wood that broke
on your beach, crates that once held herring,
freshly dead, now hold distance, nothing but the names
of the places I came from, years ago;
and you pull me from the waves,
drawing me out like a skelf,
as I would say:
a splinter.

# Albatross In Co. Antrim

*after Baudelaire*

The men would sometimes try to catch one,
throwing a looped wire at the great white cross
that tracked their every turn, gliding over their deep
gulfs and bitter waves: the bright pacific albatross.

Now, with a cardboard sign around his neck, the king
of the winds stands there, hobbled: head shorn,
ashamed; his broken limbs hang down by his side,
those huge white wings like dragging oars.

Once beautiful and brave, now tarred, unfeathered,
this lost traveller is a bad joke; a lord cut down to size.
One pokes a muzzle in his mouth; another limps past,
mimicking the *skliff, sclaff* of a bird that cannot fly.

The poet is like this prince of the clouds
who rides the storm of war and scorns the archer;
exiled on the ground, in all this derision,
his giant wings prevent his marching.

## *Lyubomir Levchev*
## The Book

The words think that I have gone to sleep.
The book falls out of my hand
the way a bird falls
from a spellbound branch.
But it doesn't fall to the floor,
in case the half-shadow is startled,
or to the sky,
in case the madness
of the zodiac is awakened.
And I
am not reading
all that anymore,
but just watching
how some book falls out
of the hand of
overtired mankind;
and remains floating
like an astronaut in weightlessness
singing of a motherland,
while she listens and knows.

Then you, darling, reach out
from the other side of things
and turn off the meaning,
whispering:
*Do you want anything else?*
*Another half-darkness?*
*Another half-sleep?*
*Another... book?*

Yes, I do.
But what is a book without love?
People want love.
Yet not half, but whole.
Even if it's sad.
Even if it's hopeless.
People want love.
So do I.
I want to read it.
I want to read it to the end.

# The Invisible Tower

Last night rained gold.
It still smells of God.

Autumn's bedding,
tumbled by passions, remains deserted.

Women look at one another – glowing.
But not knowing which one is Danaë.

Translated by Valentin Krustev and John F. Deane

# BLINDING THE SUN

*J.S.Randall*
*from* Carla

## MD 20/20

When the first plane went in she was ordering breakfast
in a diner on the upper west side – Lansky's
or the Elite she could never be sure even though
everyone was supposed to remember where they were
as for Kennedy and Martin Luther King
anyway there were people outside in the street
looking up and a hush had fallen as if
the traffic had stopped which in fact it had
and one by one the customers in the diner
went out to see what it was and none returned
or reported back but she could see them standing
on the sidewalk – a guy in a Yankees cap another
wearing an Alice Cooper Theatre of Death Tour T-shirt
a woman holding a poodle as you hold a child
arms crossed – so finally she and the counter guy
and the cook went out – they watched for a while
until the second plane went in out of nowhere
and the poodle-woman said Oh Christ
I know what this is  Life wasn't easy
for her at that time – although she'd lucked into
an illegal sub-let in SoHo and was making a living
as best she could – nights mostly – plus an occasional
money transfer from her mother – the quid pro quo
for which was a three-hour phone call – and now
she couldn't get home for the ash on lower Manhattan
so she called a friend who lived in Spanish Harlem
Mae – who said Bring something to drink
Jesus Christ I can see all the way downtown – I mean
what the fuck   They watched the news on and off

through the day and half the night – drinking – eating
microwave nachos – Mae said I woke up late
on Saturday and he'd left me a note – he's gone
LA was what he wrote but Vegas is where he's at
for sure that sonofabitch – I don't know which
he has more trouble keeping in his pants
his billfold or his pecker   Three nights she slept
on Mae's old Davenport – no-one was going
to work – they ordered in pizzas and Chinese food
and drank a lot of whisky – and smoked some good
Lebanese red – Mae had already tapped-in
to the web-cranks the conspiracy theorists the Jesus
freaks – she said You can see the Devil's face
in the smoke – so they watched it through ten times
or more – UA 175 coming into frame – the fireball
the smoke – the Prince of Darkness hollow-eyed
grinning – hanging over the city – Mae sighed
He'll be in Bellagio or Palms – some skinny whore
hanging off him – playing whatever system
he's come up with that works off what he likes to call
numerology when in fact it's nothing more
than birthdays and death days – I told him Look
even a shit-for-brains like you has got to know
a deathday will fuck your luck – whaddya think
he's probably there at the table right now
with whatever's left of my stash betting nine-eleven
Mae laughed and took a drink – she said Will you
sleep with me tonight – just company – someone to hold
is all – but we can do stuff if you like   You couldn't say
SoHo was free of it – detritus thrown about – people
crying in the street – a smell of gasoline – and this
was five days later – store-fronts darkened – plate glass
of cafes darkened – sidewalks doorways cars – she had
to move a pile of charred whatever to get
to her door – some bums had drifted over
from the East Village and made a home in the alley
across the street – they called out to her
from the depths waving their bottles of Cisco
and Wild Irish Rose – a smell of piss and liquor

to sting the back of your throat – one had his cock
in his hand – he was leaning with his forehead
against the wall waiting for something to come
another was asleep or dead – seven in all – maybe ten
someone would make a call she supposed and have
the alley emptied – it was so strange how the outrage
as Giuliani liked to call it – had lifted them
across town like hurricane wreckage left high
and dry by the sea – she crunched up a twenty
dollar bill and dropped it at her feet
as she went in and double locked and slipped
the chain across   Strange that her apartment
was just as she'd left it – well why not?
but it took her unawares as if it would be easier
to understand if stuff had been thrown around
like the time when someone had been in
for whatever he could rob to get a fix – the guy
who'd pissed on her bed and smashed some bits
and pieces but worst of all had taken her home-made
voodoo doll – not a good likeness – but she'd sewn
into it – along with a stuffing of flock – a little heart
of red silk which held hair clippings fingernail
clippings a scrap of bloodied tissue (him with his head
thrown back the tissue under his nose) that
and a word he'd used to her which she'd written out
in miniscule and folded into the little red
gris-gris bag before using blanket-stitch to seal it off
She hadn't thought to pick up anything
on her way downtown – she opened the fridge
and found some salami and rye bread and ate
standing up while she poured a Scotch – it was
OK it was fine – in the morning she'd go out
for the eggs and hash browns the lack of which
would be a 9/11 memory – that and Mae
going down on her in the dark  You could hear
sirens through the night so some time around three
she got up and went to her very own window
on the world – the hobos had lit a fire
in the alley or there *was* a fire in the alley – the flames
seemed to stretch and leap like a cat – in fact

if she half-closed her eyes it was a cat
just as Lucifer had rolled out of the smoke
from the south tower fireball or people saw the face
of Jesus bubble up on cheese-toast or the Virgin Mary
etched onto a griddle – she had once been
among a group who waited half the night for a stone
statue of the Madonna to weep as was claimed
she had and would – several nuns – a little
group of the halt and lame – a guy with a ponytail
and goatee – tourists – but the Mother of God
held out on them even though the nuns had started
a sort of serial prayer one picking up where another
left off – rosaries clacking – while the sick
and disabled looked up in misery  The bums
had finally been laid low by MD 20/20 or whatever
her twenty bucks had bought but the whole
neighbourhood was lit up as if no one could sleep
or dared to – so nothing for it but take to the streets
walk as far downtown as possible find an all-night
bar order up and think of a way to say no thanks
but as it happened he only wanted to talk about
where he'd been what he'd seen how he felt
which in order of telling were at the office
same as everyone else and like to kill
Didja see the falling man he asked – didja hear
about what they called a red mist when the bodies
hit the ground – didja catch those slo-mo
re-runs – Jesus Christ – the whole fucken thing
disappearing before your eyes – didja think
how you'd feel looking out from ninety floors up
and knowing you gotta go   The fire in the alley
had died – a line of grey was seeping into the sky
as if dawn arrived top down  She poured
a drink and thumbed a couple of Xanax
out of the blister-pack  When she closed her eyes
she saw the plane but it flew straight past – on its way
to somewhere you'd really want to go  It's time
to draw a line under this she thought – to walk away
Italy maybe – what difference – it's a throw of the dice –
birthdays or deathdays – red mist – tears from stone

## Sam Willetts
## August 9th

Down comes the squat black four tons,
drifting silent out of a virgin sky.
Forty-five seconds from release to detonation,

the sunrise-after-sunrise.
Time for millions of unexamined actions,
to finish a cup of coffee, fold your paper,

pay, leave a tip. Time too for countless moments
of conception, or destruction. Still falling;
but when the special gun inside it fires, matter

will fall apart, exponentially: *fiat lux.*
An event so bright it seems to happen many times
at once, racing to the horizons, dazzling the mind,

its moment of un-creation blinding the sun,
blowing out the walls and windows of history.
The plane that watched this all was '*Necessary Evil*'.

## *Peter Sansom*
## Petar K, 1957-2007

Despite misreading a bend and coming to
in a field you thought was death, but was only
your helmet jammed over your eyes, and laughing
that laugh of yours despite the pain, you were soon
out again testing the endless flat A-roads of Lincolnshire.
I think that's how it always was, and so it's him, not you,
I feel for, who turned unaccountably in front
of your sixty miles an hour. And what I want to say
from my safe life, my heated seats Volvo,
I want to say it's too long now, and though it's great
you liked your funeral, packed out the doors, and bringing
the sun in, *Always look on the bright side of life*,
listen Petar, isn't it time you came back? The roads
are still there with their danger right across the fens if you like,
all those roads a sea dried between islands forever
all that sea really road after road between spires,
change down for the level crossing, the patient
speed-limit in and out of a sleepy village, then go,
open her up, letting all our schoolboy years fall behind.

*Tomaž Šalamun*
# The Boats

I'm religious.
Religious as a wind or scissors.
An ant eats, she's religious, flowers are red.
I don't want to die. I don't care if I die, now.
I'm more religious than the dust in the desert.
Children's mouths are round. My eyes are
a syrup, the cold drips from it.
Sometimes I think nettles stung me, but they
didn't. I think I'm unhappy, but I'm
not.
I'm religious.
I'll throw the barrel in the river.
If bees would rush after my face, I would scratch
my face with my hand and I would see
again.
I don't get upset.
My soul presses like crowds press the door.
When I die oxen will graze the grass the same way.
Houses will glimmer the same way.


Translated by Michael Thomas Taren and the author

# *John F. Deane*
# The Hare

*for Pádraig J. Daly*

I stood, a long while, under the arms of the eucalyptus,
its nervous leaves all
biscuit-brittle, bark lifting off in strips, one space
of isolation when your being

shifts out of dailiness and focuses onto absence.
A wood-dove in the nearby grove
cooed with monotonous insistence: *tolle lege, tolle lege,*
as if the world were little more

than pages to be held up to the light. The potched
trunk of the eucalyptus rose,
a toffee-coloured column holding up the heavens
and I knew the weight of years

heavy on me, while the air of afternoon
thickened to the tolling of a bell
away over the emptied fields of the home place.
And there he was, my hare, my sweet

latchiko, white belly-bib and scut, the ears
like tablespoons filled up with snow,
watching, taut, so primed with instinctual fear I cried
that there be more than this,

more than loveliness and loss, cried for the ghosts
that are seeking still their ways
round the rush-rich meadows and pot-bellied slag-heaps
of old cottages

and these my cries, and the bell's
tolling
were silent, intense as the obdurate
growing of eucalyptus.

*Jacob Polley*
# The Work

By a lamp whose archangel's face
hangs over the earth, which is white,
and flat again, and paper, you search.
The city fills with empty light,

the desert with the little noises
with which the silence builds a church.
You like the work. I like it too.
The night sky turns from green to blue

but your whole mind is in your hand,
and how it moves and what it leaves
is world enough to understand.

Who knows the work, its tacky gleam,
the grit it sows behind the eyes,
the sleep it grants one tired of dreams?

*Katherine Gallagher*
Soundings

Track the garden
      that fields your tiger.

Track your valerian
      dreaming haywire

      and this map
      that colours you in,
      *cache-cache* offshoots.

Track your mercury,
      its lasered pulses.

Track your tree –
      its bosky spin-offs

      and your pollen –
      its chain of hours,
      daisy-fire.

Track your windmill,
      its shaky cross-bars.

Track your bridge
      (it's weigh-in time)

      and your rain-barrel,
      your precious catchment
      against quick-burn drought.

Track your diviner –
      its special water-butt.

Track your marsh,
      its wary bunyip.

Track your rain,
      its downpour grains.

## Fred D'Aguiar
## Excise

Each year I travel my passport photo
looks less like me. I feel two of us
trick our way through customs.

My heart skips a beat and I tell
myself not to breathe so shallow
when I meet a uniform blocking

my path, unlike my laminated
photo tucked in my breast pocket,
locked in amber and oblivious.

I age for both of us at double speed.
My silent partner holds his poker face,
I do all the talking for the two of us.

Nights, I dream this face but not my life,
leaving me with a sour taste and smell
and longing for a country not on any map:

to be the man who crosses borders
without a passport; whose face matches
curved lines that spell my name; no excise.

The official behind Plexiglass
takes her time to look me up and down.
I speak as she scans my passport

and watches for what the screen brings
up about me. I've no idea what she sees
that makes her ask me about my line

of work and I answer with the face
that's stranger to my passport everyday
telling lies about a life not lived, a face not his.

## Tracy Ryan
# Ramble

*for Tom Nolan*

NOW EVEN CLEARER
– sales pitch on the crazed
and peeling cover, *1999*,
the year before I left there, spine
cracked open at Cambridgeshire
as if it were an old favourite,
as if things were stuck there,
premillennial,
clearer with hindsight,
you might say, but for me it's fading.
What am I looking for?
– set of coordinates that no longer
applies, journeys you've
made & I wish
to retrace – *road atlas*
they made me repeat
in the bookstore
back when I worked there,
laughing at my "directory" –
*décalage* in the same language –
but whatever you call it, it sold
by the hundreds, & then the customer
returns, disgruntled – *my village
is missing!* – small blank, erratum
only a local would notice,
good for a refund, though presumably
they knew where it *should* be...
Unlike me, who never knew
my place, despite the discount on
Ordnance Survey Maps, where I learned
to interpret *footpath* as purely rural, interrupted
with stiles like so many valves in
a circulatory system, ha-ha and sheep grid,

hedge and drystone, understood at last
with British mud why said path must be strewn
with boot-studding stones. *Generations have trod,
have trod, have trod...* met the casual nettle and
its trite counterpart, the dock
I could never quite identify, so kept well back
despite absorbing routes in walkers' guides
I could always locate and recommend
but was never going to take, a poetics of opposites:
*LAND'S END TO JOHN O'GROATS,
ST. BEES TO ROBIN HOOD'S BAY,*
fourfold like motifs in old folk songs,
the limits spread out, mental map,
but the one I liked best, that I pored over,
gorgeously morbid: *THE LYKE WAKE WALK,*
the one on which we all, sooner or later, embark.

## Jacques Prévert
# Clocking On

Before the mill gates
the greaser starts
Summer pinches at his waist
He turns   regards
the sun
its blister of blood
grinning through clinkered sky
winks at his familiar
mutters, Comrade Sun
did you ever
find you'd lost
yet another day
to your boss?

Translated by Mario Petrucci

# BURNT-OUT LOVES NEVER RETURN

*Dannie Abse*
On Parole

Dear, so much shared. Then suddenly, solitary
confinement with the cell door half open,
sentence indefinite. After two years I dared.

You would not have liked or disliked her.
By day her sunlight lively and warming.
At night no lighthouse signalled sweet danger

and I on parole from the prison of mourning
where remembrances recur like a circle
till everything's a blur – every damn thing

a tear-blur, for we'd been utterly darned
together: knew light's secret delight: colour.
You gave me all the light you were

so to embrace another seemed a betrayal.
Not so. How could it be? But next morning
her gold was still gold – my silver, pale tinsel.

Stale, dressed in black again, I blinked at the green,
daunting, unsafe world that indisputably is,
then yours faithfully slouched back to jail.

# Postscript

Inexplicable splendour makes a man sing
as much as the pointlessness of things;

and you conceded how sweetly the wide-eyed
disfigured of the world's circus have sung
and the powdered clowns in their darkness sing.

So though late, all too late, is it demeaning
to publish love lyrics about you now?
Bitter to recall that once I pleaded,

Love, read this though it has little meaning
for by reading this you give me meaning.

## *Anne Stevenson*
# Night Thoughts, Half Dreams

Love is not a hook to hang a life on.
Not a...?
                    Well, the usual symbol
is an arrow, but that's for passion,
Cupid's feathered fire that blinds, then strips,
then leaves you naked, howling on the shingle
while Venus' shell drifts out to sea again...
a rope of hair, a hovering rosy cloak,
winds in attendance on a scalloped sea,
that fifteenth-century ripe vulgarity.


\*


Who's this appearing? Why the tears?
My first piano teacher, Mrs. Efron,
beloved and forgotten    sixty years

crying for lost Petersburg    lost Schumann
*Kinderszenen* never to return...
crying so hard I creep out from my lesson
crying. Nine years old. And yesterday.


\*


Yesterday    Monday    May Bank Holiday.
Those all-but-dead crack willows by the river,
rising from trashy water in green tracery.

That tiny girl, her black braids flapping,
skip-roping over the puddles on the path,
skipping for the sake of skipping.


\*

When tears at last drowned Julia Efron, she
forgot about teaching me to play.
For a while she stalked our upper storey...
scary at night, a shadow walking.
Waking, I heard the floorboards cry.
Then she disappeared, leaving me,
tenderly inscribed, *The Story of Painting*.

So I met and fell in love with Botticelli
whose ladies I envied for their floating clothes,
wondering at the incandescent flowery nakedness
in which they posed...

Though none were lovelier than Mrs. Efron,
wishbone thin and olive skinned,
hair smoothed back into a coal black bun.

'*And for what, except for you, do I feel love?*'

She smiles at me
through tears with rainbows in them.

*Jane Holland*
# The Ritz In The Seventies

In the corner suite my mother lay prostrate
on the chaise longue, a twenty-stone
Josephine. The flowery tent
of her dress was nylon, fawn tights
and espadrilles, oddly Peruvian.

Buses passed outside in the dusk; Green Park
misty below us, luminescent
in semi-darkness. My father sat
in a cream silk, stiff-backed armchair,
moustachioed and taciturn,
reading his newspaper. *The Times*, no doubt,
though they'd let their standards slip
since he was there.

In those days, I was allowed to go out
unaccompanied, as far as Hatchards
at least, or the gusty steps down
to the Tube. Back in the suite, I ordered
Beef Wellington with horseradish
and danced about like a Bohemian, barefoot,
watching myself in cream-framed mirrors.

## *Rita Ann Higgins*
## He Was No Lazarus

In the newsagents come bric-a-brac
days were spent gawking out
hoping the girls would come in for a chat
or any old gossip that would help throttle
a jaded afternoon.

I smoked nearly as many cigarettes as I sold
and what I didn't sell, I gave away.
The Shantalla gang came in ones and twos
'give us a fag loveen' and I'd give them twenty.

Once I gave Elvis Kelly a yo-yo
to pass the time until he went to England.
I'll give you one long snake kiss for it, he said.
They all went to England on the half-three out of Galway.
We were like banshees crying over them
then we lived for the S.W.A.L.K. letters.

Harlesden got him and plenty more besides;
he drowned his sorrows in The Green Man.
A right yo-yo, he fell under his own weight and broke his skull.
A maverick blood vessel made the same noise as a cork
pop went his flash lights and he all fell down.

When he went down he stayed down, ton of bricks style,
he was no Lazarus, no shape changing Greek or Roman god
no comic book super villain who could say,
Abra Kadabra now you see me now you don't.

He was no Zossima either, though he wore the brown
scapular of our lady of Mount Carmel around his neck.
He came home in a box, spartan no frills
just a shiny plate with his name, his date of birth.

I was one long snake kiss out of pocket.

*Carol Rumens*
# Diphthongs

In labour you grow old
you listen to the pain   you give it room
  to stretch a little wider and a little
                    wider till it tears a noise from you
that's not the child unless
                    the child is pain.


You're interested at first   surprised to learn
  nature has set no limits
  your body   though you love it   sets no limits
      but tricks you with a little
      easy pain that's the beginning of
                a wave that won't stop gathering when you say
                                enough
                      fold back   give over


pain doesn't hesitate because a forehead
        shines or breath is
        harsh. Pain has its say   it burns
  enormous holes through prayers. *Pain will learn you*.


There are such diphthongs in the word   pain
                you're opening like the future
                            and all it says is death
and death's like this
                perhaps
                  or dying is.


But this
  time it's not death. Remember
the other meaning   breathe it   rhyme it further
        and harder   wider   harder                    till wide nature
    is satisfied   closes her golden eye
          relents. Your turn.
                    You turn

you turn towards
     the little wounded human face   the only
      the only vowel   and shining
           there's no limit to your shining.

## *Maureen Duffy*
## Mammicks

'Obsolete', the dictionary dubs it or, lip curling, 'dialect'.
Cold meat on Monday, shepherded into pie on Tuesday
or sandwiched into my uncle's lunchbox
bubble-and-squeaked on Wednesday with last night's
cold mashed; Thursday was stew or steak-and-kidney
pudding and we were glad to have said
goodbye to the mammicks, a word that came down the line
to start a new life in the smoke for another century.

When I find it again, made classy by Shakespeare
and scholarship, meaning 'cut in little pieces,
leftovers', it still has the tag 'origin obscure',
an old word for old ways now warmed up again
as the cold bites, though the words themselves
buried under fast-food technospeak
like burnt-out loves never return.

*Nov. 17th 2008*

# THOSE WHO PASS AWAY

*Tim Liardet*
*from* The Storm House

## 2

Sequestered brother, a year dead, now the world
must get by without you. If once you had willed
world and self into being, and looked for their limit, now
the world vaporizes with the self. Let's say
you're further from home than me tonight. Out here,
estranged from my own life, I've the space to confer
with your rather untalkative absence. It might be
a sort of praying, or a speaking of terms which will
remove me further and further from the lobby:
the noise is far below, now that I've slipped away
and have to lift the dicky bar of the fire door
to retreat to my room, until a time rain through the glass
streams, like a ghost, over the hotel letterhead
which was never once intended to address the dead.

## 7

The two policemen, seven foot tall, came to tell
our mother you were dead – their overcoats dripped along
The Acorns' newly polished corridor before their words,
spoken softly, released the flash-flood of her grief
which set her arms flailing and ornaments flying
as she moved to knock the lanky messengers
on their backs on the slab where you lay, feet splayed.
A straitjacket was considered, but how could a bodice
that anchored her hands, a grope of straps, constrain
out-of-body grief? The constables read their shoes,
and news of your death reached as far as it would get.
*Fishy*, said our beautiful Asian doctor, to the pharmacist
who said the same to the salesgirl, who seemed to say
such fishiness could already smell the sea.

## 11

*Unprovoked*, said our mother, the attack on you
a month before you died – the death before the death:
the stave with six inch nails driven through it
clutching the flesh of your back like the scourge's hooks
as you hugged your knees for protection;
as if those spikes tilling the soil of your back
were not considered a clue, as if wounds
more terrible, more disfiguring, might have been a clue.
Though these wounds appalled the doctor they drew
the mandatory nod, the shrug of the police:
this was the way you were taught the imperatives
of justice in this world, how each nail which could
have punctured wrist and ankle had not spared
an inch of flesh against your broken word.

## 23

The stick came down from every angle,
there were twenty, no, thirty sticks, each seen from another angle,
each coming down empowered by the reason
for its own force, more vehemence here for this
less vehemence here for that, some regret here,
some grief, some asking-for-forgiveness,
but in that moment, I do believe, most sticks imagined her
sat in a wicker chair on some Bolivian balcony
watching insects over water, comfortable she was too far
from her sins to be blamed. And the damage done
by the blow, you were convinced, was a kind
of suitable punishment, a sort of justice.
It was justice that was energy, justice that was fuel;
it was justice that put the whip in the ferule.

## 25

Like something that cannot help but move
however injured, appalled, however hurt,
she climbed back to her feet. Raskolnikov's nightmare –
the old woman rising from the puddle of her blood.
And this the strange thing – the blow which had felled her
in the very manner it had been delivered came back,
came back, came back and struck you across the head
and split the skin of your cranium, blue bruises bloomed
all across your torso, and the pressure which
the blow had released was pushed back
into the chamber which created it, but worse now,
cramping your muscles. The blow came back, and almost
wrenched out from its socket the very arm
which had delivered it, sent back to where it started from.

## 31

The nights pour over and are not themselves
and where has she been, for all those hours? Wandering
in her nightdress, to the bottom of the garden
where just for a moment she might have seen you
where just for a moment she saw you
where she saw you, she says, like the Batalha Christ
– all torso, blown away at the knees –
visible only from the waist up, looking straight ahead;
where she saw you, she says, forming and unforming
in the vapours of low blood sugar, standing stock-still
and relenting from under the firs into a sort
of smile, a sense of the yet-to-be-assembled
weighting the darkness behind the ash-cans
and weighing, weighing in your punctured hands.

## Gerald Dawe
## Déjà-vu

*Each day's light has more significance these days.*
— Frank O'Hara

*in memory of Terence Chartres Bradshaw*

I should say first of all that the Bank of Ireland
on the corner of North Street next to where your pal
Carly's mother ran the photographic studio
we all went to for annual portraits until that stopped,
in the sixties, that that wonderful art-deco
building is closed and boarded-up, the doors
scrawled over – what do you expect after
all the war and mayhem? – and the Grand Central Hotel

you used to frequent in the snazziest of snazzy suits,
the film star look – it went years ago, alas,
replaced by the dire shopping mall, no GPO,
no grand hotel, just the date stones of buildings,
laid in the nineteenth century when the city was all gothic,
and your Mother and Father were conceived and started
to make their way towards each other, and by the time
you came about, the wars began, 'The less said the better'.

Now, a short life later, at the drop of a hat,
a mere seventy years on, you go and bow out on us,
the messenger boy, the only boy entrant, the spark, the dancer,
the chatter-upper, the dab hand, the butterfly, the only boy
you go and push off with no fly-past, no Dam Busters,
but an unceremonious last tour, to your old school,
your old buddies, like boys again in the Forces,
the white cuffs showing just so, the quiff,

the breast pocket handkerchief,
and always the laugh, (the jaded look came later),
sitting where I am now, your feet jive
to the music of time, swivelling this way and that,
on the steps one day of the Central Library
you approached me and my mates –
'My uncle Terry', a whiff of drink taken in McGlade's,
your grandfather's spot, or Hercules of the Horseshoe Bar.

Daydreams and marijuana in the Waterworks,
tripping down Limestone Road,
the RUC band playing in Alexander Park,
lying stretched out in the Grove,
for that was the Summer of Love,
blue skies all the way from Napoleon's Nose to Scrabo,
cadging admission to the Small Faces,
Pink Floyd in the Ulster Hall, Hendrix in the Whitla,

'All along the Watchtower' – and hearing your step in late,
about four in the morning, the light in the back room
had started to spill from ceiling to floor,
in your wake, cigarette smoke and aftershave
like it was only yesterday: women pushing huge prams,
men in suits with lunch boxes and, of course,
*The Sky at Night*, which I will never forget,
from my little perch, my secret eyrie at the top of the house.

But no one asked after you, or said Hello,
they just kept on – and who would blame them,
in the squalls of rain before the sunlight came
along with a sudden gust up North Street and down by
discount shops and ragged car parks and the view
all the way to where we once lived like everyone else,
or so we thought, swimming away in our own underworld,
the Czech vase in the bay window, the sun-blinds,

the grandfather clock on the landing, waking up
in arctic bedrooms to milky skies and freezing mornings,
everyone heading to work, on packed buses –
could it have been so, through autumn and winter,
spring and summer? – women sitting on spruce porches
in behind their front gardens and the kids,
like a breed unto themselves, hanging out down the back,
when the nights lengthened and you'd arrive in,

from somewhere very different than this orderly world
that's gone now – like you collapsed in a heap
on the bathroom floor, like you horsing up the stairs,
like you acting the lig, 'Who goes there?',
like the pop of the gas-fire being lit in granny's bedroom,
the white columns that turned sky-blue,
the scraggy nights of racing clouds,
the kitchen lights going on, one after another,

at the same time, the shadows on the ceiling,
the shining car parked where it shouldn't have been,
the sound of someone whistling down the lane
and the whole thing starting up all over again,
every morning without fail, come sun, rain or hail,
without you or I, without the blink of an eye,
the blinds drawn for mourning –
that's what should have been done,

all the way down the gardens and avenues,
just for you who'd sailed through,
smoozing with the best of them until demob' came
with the banner WELCOME HOME
and you're back on Civvy Street...
That day I swear I saw you all of a sudden,
the weather turned from foul storm-cloud
to brilliant sunshine like a flash of light

and in a second gone as we beetled along
to the megastores in one-time fashion houses,
the fast food outlets on the mosaic ground floors,
the medical hall, the Ulster Club, the Scottish Prudential,
the red brick luminous in the falling rain,
stumbling up the stairs in fits of laughter,
gone like all the people dressed for the part,
gone like a ship slipping out to sea into the dark,

gone like that Easter break, rolling eggs down
the hillside until they smashed into smithereens,
the long silence of Sunday afternoons,
the fog horns blasting in the New Year,
the slow erosions of that life into fear
by which time you had well and truly gone,
and what remains, who can ever tell? –
to see it all again – the turning in a street corner,

the light on a landing, a door that was never
quite flush, the names cut one summer
in the softened flashing of the top window,
and all the things that seem the same,
moonlight on rooftop, the shouted question,
a slow silhouetted figure that moves
across the blinds, the brazen air of early spring
as everything becomes new once more.

## Jeri Onitskansky
## If This Rings True

like a rock
thrown a certain angle into water, and becomes
circles of water, maybe
some heaviness ripples-up-against
leaping –
recognition sinking
in deep among fish-shadows?

## Linda Maria Baros
## The Lake Of Dyer's Madder

Those who pass away, nearly transparent, nearly weightless –
        you can make out their bloated remains
        through the lake of dyer's madder bandages –,
those who pass away, it's well known, must walk
        through olive boughs, like linen
        undulating in the air. They breach barriers
        with their breasts and keep on walking.
Their iris looks like a door slammed shut,
        a fallen bolt, a prison cell.
        They want to tell us something with their earthen lips
        before the lava of their face, darkening to purple,
        fades forever.

Those who pass away thus walk on and on through the night's gold
                                                        gardens,
like parents who don't even once contrive to cast their eyes
        behind them.

Translated by Adam J. Sorkin and George Volceanov with the poet

# FULL LENGTH PORTRAITS

I remember at the end, after reading poem after poem
about death urges, abortion and torrid love affairs, she
stood in the limelight kissing her hands to her cheering
audience before accepting a huge bouquet of red roses.
— *Anne Stevenson on Anne Sexton*

# Anne Sexton Forty Years Later

Charlotte Austin questions Anne Sexton's contemporary, Anne Stevenson, about her view of this poet's importance and the effect her work has had on woman's poetry and the women's movement after Sexton's suicide in 1974.

*How did you first discover Anne Sexton?*
Anne Sexton was big news to American students of poetry in 1960-61, when, after marriage and divorce in England, I'd returned to the University of Michigan to study for an MA in English with the poet, Donald Hall. Sexton's first book, *To Bedlam and Part Way Back*, had just been published. W.D. Snodgrass, whom I met through Hall, had paved the way to "confessional poetry" with his post-divorce *Heart's Needle* shortly before; Robert Lowell soon followed suit with *Life Studies*, and Hall, I think, was as surprised and impressed as I was by these developments. Free-flowing, autobiographical writing like this was a radical departure from the craftsman-like poetry of Richard Wilbur, who – more my contemporary than Yeats, Eliot and Frost – had been my primary exemplar up to that time. I must have become aware of poets like Lowell, Snodgrass, Sexton, Plath, Adrienne Rich, in the same year that I discovered the poems of Elizabeth Bishop. Before 1960 I wrote poetry tentatively, full of self-doubt. After 1961, with the encouragement of Donald Hall, I began to indulge my ambition.

*Did you meet her? Did you ever see her perform her poetry on stage?*
I think I met Anne Sexton once (before she was famous), after a reading I was part of myself at the Hebrew Youth Centre in New York. That would have been in the winter of 1959-60, when I was living in the upper 90s with my first husband and small daughter. I had joined a writing workshop at the YHA, with Stanley Kunitz, and I attended readings there whenever I could. Then, much later, maybe in 1970, I heard her read at the 'Y' alone – horrified, I have to say, at the way she produced herself. I remember at the end, after reading poem after poem about death urges, abortion and torrid love affairs, she stood in the limelight kissing her hands to her cheering audience before accepting a huge bouquet of red roses. That performance put her out of court for me for a long time.

*I'd like to know what particularly intrigues you about her life and work.*
Well, after that extremely exhibitionist reading, I decided I didn't like her

work at all, but I still had to admit that her first collections affected me. She and Sylvia Plath together, in effect, had given me permission to write about my own divorce and family discontents. Being me, though, and by that time strongly under the influence of Elizabeth Bishop, I had already decided to deflect the stream of my own troubles and write from an historical perspective. So I concocted a story, out of nineteenth and twentieth century family letters (some of them my own family's), called *Correspondences*; in which I tried to show how a twentieth century woman from a privileged Christian middle-class American family could well have found it in her to embrace madness and suicide as desirable alternatives to safe domestic frustration. It wasn't Anne Sexton's talent (which was real enough) or her mental illness (also real) that intrigued me. It was why that talent could only be developed when driven in tandem, so to speak, with a personal death wish. Why were so many women poets of the sixties and seventies driven crazy by their roles as women? I never myself went mad, but I suffered a good deal from the same syndrome of acute misery, unhappy in my roles of daughter, wife, lover and mother.

*You say you don't consider yourself to have belonged to the women's movement – although you were writing during this period. What do you think Sexton contributed to the movement?*

Well, I don't like gender distinctions. I felt then, and still feel, much as Elizabeth Bishop did about not shackling one's art to any pre-set social or political programme. I'm sure, though, that both Anne Sexton and Sylvia Plath contributed vitally to the women's movement by appearing to be talented, oppressed women prepared to die for liberation – though this was not true of either one. What does seem to be the case is that they made possible a great deal of today's poetry written by women. Sylvia died in 1963, before the movement really got under way, but Sexton was delighted that so many women artists caught fire from her example. Mind you, Sexton's egotistical drive was much stronger than her gender loyalty or social conscience. Though it may sound unkind to say this, having read Diane Middlebrook's biography, I suspect Sexton was never mentally healthy enough to engage deeply – for all her many lovers – with anyone except herself. That for eight years she chiefly corresponded with herself through thrice-weekly visits to her psychotherapist means that she was miserably aware of her extreme self-centeredness and hated herself bitterly because of it. That polarized self-love and self-hatred, I suppose, was the sickness snarled at the centre of her.

*What was your reaction to her poetry at this time? Were you inspired, intimidated, offended, liberated?*

First intimidated, then offended. But, to be fair, probably liberated and inspired at the same time; my feelings about her in the sixties/seventies were in confusion, just as they were, more importantly for me, about Sylvia Plath.

*Has your response to her work changed over time?*

Yes, I'm much more tolerant now than I was; I pity her, but I'm certainly not envious or resentful, as I suppose I used to be. I simply don't find her poetry nourishing. It's all too much the same. That unvaried tone of furious self-pity gets me down – though I admit I am impressed, sometimes, with the poems' imaginative richness and flow. She worked hard on her poems, and she made them work for her. I used to be dismissive of her talent; I now think, considering how much she depended on it, that she would have died much sooner had her gift not been so strong, conspicuous and instantly popular.

*Her style changed over the years, can you comment on this?*

Yes, unfortunately the kind of self-expressionist poetry she believed in was not susceptible of further development. Sexton wanted to be remembered as a great poet, and she tried increasingly to amplify her passion for death by plunging into relationships with religion and God. In my view, her poems aren't capable of approaching the self-renunciation any deep religious belief demands. Poor Anne, her last two or three books are so desperately misjudged as to tone, over-painted in glow-colours with sexy images. No wonder even the most sympathetic of priests wouldn't consider her bid to become a Roman Catholic.

*Do you have a particular collection, style or theme which you are most drawn to?*

Yes, I think her early books, *To Bedlam and Part Way Back* and *All My Pretty Ones*, are her most satisfying. She's best when she slightly makes fun of her own bravura, as in her signature poem, 'Her Kind'. 'The Truth the Dead Know', written after her parents' death, is a beautiful poem, as is the title poem of *All My Pretty Ones*. Her hospital poems, 'The Operation' and 'The Abortion', work effectively through impressive rhythmic patterns. One of my enduring favorites, 'Old' is not about herself but tenderly describes a fellow patient. I love its last line, "In a dream you are never eighty."

*Can you a choose a poem and talk to me about it from an academic point of view, by which I mean its structure, the style she uses? I'm interested in her poems in this way, as well as in the emotional reaction people have to her work. I want to know how 'good' they were with reference to the craft.*

The poems in Sexton's first two books were largely written in workshop conditions in the late fifties and early sixties, first under John Holmes and later under Robert Lowell. It's interesting to see how carefully she structured them. Look at the first verse of 'Old Dwarf Heart' from *All My Pretty Ones* in which she establishes a six-line stanza, rhythmically free though carefully end rhymed, *abccba*:

> When I lie down to love,
> old dwarf heart shakes her head.
> Like an imbecile she was born old.
> Her eyes wobble as thirty-one thick folds
> of skin open to glare at me on my flickering bed.
> She knows the decay we're made of.

Dylan Thomas, as well as Robert Lowell, in those days provided models choosing outlandish images and then guiding them syntactically through a controlled form. Sexton's stanza here consists of four simple sentences in which the only obscure reference – "thirty-one thick folds / of skin" – must refer to the poet's age. Under a critical microscope, this fourth line with its enjambment looks and sounds wrong. Even when I was beginning to write, I would never have allowed myself to rhyme *old* with *folds*. That supposed central rhyme ought to be the strongest, but the plural 's' weakens it. Sexton makes what to me is the same mis-sound in the third stanza, rhyming a second line "And worse, the sores she *holds*" with a fifth line, "she is all red muscle, humming in and out, *cajoled* / by time". The clumsiness of that "*holds / cajoled*" rhyme is especially noticeable because the first and last lines chime perfectly: "Good God, the things she *knows*" with "Where I go, she *goes*." The final stanza turns on a middle rhyme of "wrists" (plural) and "fist" (singular), but the sound-strain there is not so noticeable, with those similar "ists". Unfortunately, by this time, her subject heart seems to be neither flesh nor soul, (a heart, like a fist, unfolding its arms and wrists?) and when the poem veers off into genealogy, it leaves me, I'm afraid, puzzled and disappointed. Here is the final stanza (the "seventy coats" at the end must refer back to the "thirty-one skins" of age in the first stanza):

Oh now I lay me down to love,
how awkwardly her arms undo,
how patiently I untangle her wrists
like knots. Old ornament, old naked fist,
even if I put on seventy coats I could not cover you...
mother, father, I'm made of.

It may be unfair to pick on this less known, rather awkward example of her work, yet it seems to me typical of what so often goes wrong in it. Like many of Sexton's poems, this one runs all right, but when you look at it critically, you see it's missing a couple of cylinders. Form, matter and rhythm are at odds, and the novel image of an "old dwarf heart" can't hold it together.

*Can you comment on the main themes of her work – what do they tell us about her preoccupations?*
Anne Sexton's chief preoccupation was her own sickness and love affair with death. Thanks to her psychotherapist, her addiction to suicide drove her to poetry. Self-hatred, frenetic efforts to find love through sex, resentment of her parents (chiefly her mother), fear, self-doubt, ambition to become a celebrity poet – all these were preoccupations. To me, such intensely selfish and subjective obsessions in an adult are at bottom childish – sick, maybe forgivable, but childish. This is why today her poems sound an enduring voice of permanent adolescence. Such a voice is naturally attractive to actual adolescents, who happily flock to horror movies, pop stars and crazy disco music. To adults, Anne's poems can sound pathetically sad; maybe even ridiculous to the elderly.

It seems clear now that America itself was going through a prolonged period of adolescence after World War II. How many European and Russian civilians died in that war? The historian Norman Davis gives a death-figure of twenty seven million, and that's excluding the six million Jews killed in the Holocaust and the Japanese killed by the atomic bomb in Hiroshima and Nagasaki. Meanwhile, the USA and Canada reclined on the other side of the Atlantic, young, rich, strong, and untouched except possibly by guilt and almost certainly by immaturity. Both Sexton and Plath began to publish in the early 60s, when literary America itself was pretty crazy. Fashionable psychotherapy was probably a good deal to blame, although it's hard to say whether the intellectual craze for craziness preceded or followed the infectious popularity of Freudian psychoanalysis.

Note, though, that I am *not* saying Sexton was faking; nor were Delmore

Schwarz, John Berryman, Theodore Roethke and Sylvia Plath. Poets, artists in general in a sick culture are like canaries in a mine full of poison gas, the first to suffer.

*Do you feel her work is a kind of documentary of her life?*
Yes, of course. Anne Sexton's is one of the great American stories of successful failure. If you can't succeed at success, succeed at failing. But I'm afraid both her life story and her bold confessional poetry opened the way to a great deal of inferior writing today. Snodgrass, Lowell, Sexton and Plath between them set an example, for men as well as women, of what I call 'therapoetry' – poetry written mainly for therapeutical purposes. Not all such poetry is bad, of course. Some of Lowell's and Plath's is superb, and a lot is very affecting, very appealing. Still, it reverses the priorities of art. Wordsworth, W.B. Yeats, T.S. Eliot could transform their personal feelings into memorably impersonal works by drawing the mind away from the sordid miseries of their lives into what Yeats called (suspending disbelief, of course) "the artifice of eternity". They aimed to create the kind of beauty that Bach achieved in his *Preludes* and *Fugues* and Vermeer in his Dutch interiors. Reality, in the best art, is neither escaped nor ignored but expressed in a transmuted form. And this, for me, is the best therapy. I don't need to create it myself; I only need to give myself to its sympathy and understanding. Important art, it seems to me, *looks out* at the world, achieves a perspective *beyond* its immediate chaos and cruelty. Therapoetry looks inward like psychoanalysis and seeks to uncover the poisonous sewers buried in the mind – sewers indeed in need of cleaning by painful exposure, but not there for poets to wallow in for fear of finding, upon recovery, that they no longer are inspired to write.

*It was her therapist who suggested that Sexton write poetry in order to help her to cope with her mental health issues. What do you think about this suggestion? At the time would it have been a revolutionary treatment?*
Then? Certainly revolutionary. After reading Diane Middlebrook's biography, I can't believe Anne Sexton would have written poetry without her therapist's encouragement. She owed Dr. Orne a great debt of gratitude, and she knew it. It was when, after eight years, he left Boston and she twice attempted to change her doctor, that she found herself stranded in an unsupported life-situation, *sans* Dr. Orne, who had become her surrogate father, and *sans* her husband, whom she had divorced. You can't read Sexton's story without being full of sympathy for her husband Keyo's long-suffering loyalty throughout their fraught marriage. And then one day he comes home from

work, and there's Anne, drunk in the sitting room, demanding a divorce! So, apart from women friends like Maxine Kumin, she had no one at the end to coddle her.

*Some say that poetry saved her life (for a while anyway). How much would you agree with this statement?*
Yes, this is almost certainly the case. She saw poetry and suicide as the positive and negative poles of her life... as she said coherently in her memoir of Sylvia Plath. I suspect most British readers don't know that Anne Sexton, five years older than Plath, was famous in America well before Plath appeared on the scene. The two poets met in Robert Lowell's writing seminar in 1959. Sexton used to drive Plath and an escort – the poet George Starbuck – to The Boston Ritz after class. There, over "three or four or two martinis" the girls would "talk at length, and in depth" about their suicides. Plath's journal suggests they were friendly rivals before, in the early sixties, Sexton's first two books were greeted by sensational reviews. Plath's *The Colossus* had to wait for recognition. When, in Devon, Plath received from Sexton a copy of *All My Pretty Ones*, she obviously was impressed enough to let its influence seep into the unrestrained and for those times shocking tone of poems like 'Daddy' and 'Medusa'.

*Sexton received psychiatric treatment for much of her life. Some people have said that the treatment she received was detrimental both to her mental health and to her later poetry. What are your thoughts on the effects of therapy on her poetry and on its chance of lasting in the future?*
Dr. Orne contributed a preface to Middlebrook's biography in which he ascribes the collapse of her personality and her eventual suicide to his own "desertion" of her when he left Boston for a job in Philadelphia. I don't know, of course, but my suspicion is that she would have killed herself even had Dr. Orne remained on hand to hold her hand and tape her sessions. As to how long her poems will out last her life story? Five or six poems will endure, perhaps, like Dylan Thomas's. I could be wrong, but it seems likely that Anne Sexton will be remembered mainly for her influence in bringing about that interesting age of psychoanalysis and infectious insanity that in the 1960s and 70s utterly changed the direction and texture of American poetry.

# Don Paterson: *Rain*, Etc

SEAN O'BRIEN

*I have never been quite certain that one should be more than an artist* [...]
— W.B.Yeats, *What is "Popular Poetry"?*

Few poets can have covered as much ground in twenty years as Don Paterson. Talk of a poet's 'development' often concerns the discovery of 'a voice' which is then explored, refined and, perhaps, ultimately exhausted in self-parody. This can involve the process of stylization of which Randall Jarrell accused Auden in a famous essay.[1] In our own period, to choose a couple of examples at random, the process of refinement can be seen (and no criticism is implied in these cases) in the work of Peter Reading, and that of exhaustive exploration in the late Peter Redgrove. At their various stages of development, the poets named sound unmistakeably, and increasingly, like themselves, and this can be interpreted as both a power and a problem. In contrast, re-reading the six books Don Paterson has published to date suggests that a significant part of his work involves a process of attempted self-cancellation, a shedding of particulars in pursuit of a final adaptability. If Auden, Reading and Redgrove are idiosyncratic, Paterson is attempting to escape a voice and a signature as though to acquire the authority of anonymity, in line with Machado's contention that "my feeling is not only mine, *but ours*".[2] Such an effort may stand behind Paterson's conviction that poetry "proceeds not from a selfish but a generous instinct." Neither approach is necessarily superior; both are inescapably rhetorical (abnegation itself tends to characterize its exponent, for example); but Paterson's is the more unusual. No doubt Paterson, no stranger to Scottish originalism, would find grounds for distinguishing his procedures from Eliot's attempt at impersonality.

I'm not a musician, but it seems that this attempted divestment of work from the self has similarities with a sense of music as a permanent event rather than an individual composition, a sense familiar to a player like Paterson who has worked in the crossover between traditional music and jazz. There are obvious limitations to the analogy here: music does also get

---

1. 'Changes of Attitude and Rhetoric in Auden's Poetry', *The Third Book of Criticism* (1975).
2. *Times Alone: Selected Poems of Antonio Machado*, translated by Robert Bly (1983, p.6). All references to Bly's versions of Machado are to this volume.

composed as well as inherited or improvised; the self is not shed simply because the self wishes it; but some of the most important and interesting strands in Paterson's work to date reveal a process of purgation, and to follow its development results in an enhanced awareness of how serious the claims he makes for poetry actually are (though this is not, of course, the only thing his poems are doing.) His practice runs very close to his theory, which in his essay 'The Lyric Principle Part 1: The Sense of Sound' aims to demonstrate that poetry is the natural and inevitable condition of language, so that (we may infer) there is no need to argue defensively that it is a human necessity.[3]

At the same time as Paterson's own work undertakes an increasingly strict rationing of 'personality', his metaphysical cast of mind and imagination leads to a much firmer assertion that poetry is a mode of knowledge than perhaps we are accustomed to. Could this metaphysical turn have been foretold on the evidence of Paterson's first collection, *Nil Nil* (1993)? From hints and gestures, to some degree. In hindsight, though, *Nil Nil* is more clearly than ever a young man's book, teeming with possibilities but at least as much concerned with achieving formal authority as with subject matter. Hence perhaps the dozen strenuous sonnets, whose subject seems as much the discovery, establishment and maintenance of their own order as anything else: the reader overhears a struggle in progress. Paterson's approach is very different from some of his contemporaries: Glyn Maxwell's forms can provoke him to bravura elaboration, while Simon Armitage often uses form as an approximation against which the voice is free to play. In Paterson, however, the embrace of constraint is part of the contract between form and imagination. Paterson's early masters were Mahon and Muldoon, though he rarely resembles either very much, but his exemplar was surely a poet of the immediately senior generation, Michael Donaghy, the poet as conjuror, whose enviable technical assurance meant that in the first place the reader's attention seemed to be firmly directed at subject matter. It may well have been to this end that Paterson's labours were directed.

*Nil Nil* is also teeming with *stuff*. Its world is enormously detailed, recalling the encyclopaedism of Peter Didsbury's work, for example, whose principle of inclusion lends the poet a world-making power. There is the pool game in 'The Ferryman's Arms', or the lovingly minute account of the slow extinction of a football team in the title poem, or the random but paranoically careful itemizing of books in 'The Alexandrian Library'. The last is a long, Borgesian piece which seems fuelled by an authorial anxiety that

---

3. 'The Lyric Principle Part 1: The Sense of Sound', *Poetry Review*, 97:2.

something might have been left out of a poem/library which is by definition both exhaustive and incomplete, finite but unlimited. It is, as it were, not the vast silence of the cosmic library that worries Paterson so much as the sense that a book may be overdue. At this stage, though, metaphysical paradox seems attractive rather than a real cause for crisis, a bit like taking half a tab of acid rather than the whole thing.

While *God's Gift to Women* (1997) broaches painful material, its air seems clearer, its varieties of line each more assured. Consider the flexible couplets of 'Prologue', the tiny rhymed quatrains of '00:00: Law Tunnel', and in particular the octosyllabic couplets of the title poem, in which the study of Mahon's and Lowell's study of Marvell has paid off, allowing constraint to generate its own slowing of time, and within it room for manoeuvre:

> even now, at your martyrdom
> the window, loose inside its frame,
> rolls like a drum, but at the last
> gives out, and you give up the ghost.
> Meanwhile our vernacular
> Atlantis slides below the stars:
> My Lord's Bank, Carthagena, Flisk,
> Go one by one into the dusk.

Somewhere in the background of this stanza lies the proposal made in Douglas Dunn's exquisite 'Loch Music', from *St Kilda's Parliament* (1981): "[...] I am not administered / Tonight but feel my life transferred / Beyond the realm of where I am / Into a personal extreme, / As on my wrist, my eager pulse / Counts out the blood of someone else." Reading Dunn's poem as part of an *ars poetica* for a moment, it seems the readiness is all: discipline – the management, the naturalization of form – offers an anticipation of a broad freedom, a passport into the sphere of the poetic (construed as the natural environment), where creating and being created merge in the task of remaking the base material of experience in the image of an understanding. Elsewhere, in 'Reading Pascal in the Lowlands', from *Elegies* (1985), Dunn describes himself as "light with meditation, religiose / And mystic with a day of solitude", disposed to the religious but not adhering to it: like it or not, there is a residual religious element in Paterson's work too. Where his friend Donaghy lapsed from Catholicism but retained its sense of scale and order, Paterson fell away from Pentecostalism while seeming to take with him a comparable appetite for totalizing depictions of human experience – hence perhaps the Borges, the sonnets, the preoccupation with Fibonacci numbers and the golden mean, and, especially, the refusal to countenance the idea that words are only signs, phantoms of meanings and objects.

Translation is a natural development for Paterson's work. After the version from Rimbaud and from an imaginary poet in *Nil Nil*, it becomes a primary concern in *The Eyes* (1999), a book which is subtitled "a version of Antonio Machado" and further described on the cover as "lying somewhere between translation and imitation". Given that none of these terms is of watertight exactitude, it seems that Paterson is, like many another, seeking to extricate himself from some of the obligations accepted (and at times enforced) by some translators and scholars. Exact fidelity to form and meaning gives place to the exploration of imaginative common ground – the effort, as Paterson puts it in his Afterword, "to write the poem Machado is for me, the one about God and love and memory". The outcome is intended to work as a poem in English rather than to offer an apologetic or shadowy gesture at the original (an approach whose results often tend to be 'true' but not interesting). The process, of course, aligns Paterson with much modernist practice and is of a piece with his determined dismissal of the claims of various avant-garde tendencies to be the true inheritors of modernism.

That he applies this approach to Machado enables him to begin the metaphysical turn in earnest, and the reader notes Paterson's observation that "I can think of no other writer so obsessed with the suppression of his own ego". A little later, describing his "versions", Paterson speaks of his wish "to plead with the reader to forget the relation in which these poems stand to the originals", the thrust being that the author of the versions should likewise be permitted to disappear and be removed from the account. The poem is, allegedly, to constitute its own history.

Paterson's attachment to Machado enables him to inherit a vocabulary of fundamentals – such as road, sea, sun, night, sleep – on which to build a series of variations. 'Siesta' derives from 'Siesta: in Memory of Abel Martin', Machado's imaginary poet. If we compare Paterson's version with that of Robert Bly, an early champion of Machado, what we find (not unexpectedly, given the poets involved) is a poem less roseate and pious than Bly's, less inclined to give place to the presumed 'voice' of the original. Paterson works in two rhyming octets, the tone businesslike and even peremptory:

> To the God of absence and of aftermath,
> of the anchor in the sea, the brimming sea…
> whose truant omnipresence sets us free

from this world, and firmly on the one true path,
with our cup of shadows overflowing, with
our hearts uplifted, heavy and half-starved,
let us honour Him who made the Void, and carved
these few words from the thin air of our faith.

The paradoxes are decisively rendered here, hard-edged and right-angled, for the Anglophone reader. For one thing, the poet is still living on premises from which faith has been evicted. The word "faith" stands in for the original's "*razon*", reason. For the Catholic Church, reason is a divinely-given faculty whose ultimate function is to show that faith is the ultimate rational act – a process enforced by doctrine and hierarchical authority, the dead letter evoked in Bly's version of 'Tenue rumor de tunicas que pasan': "Faint sound of robes brushing / the exhausted earth! / And so much grief / from the ancient bells." Paterson, though, seems to approach from the direction of a Protestant conviction that individual engagement with scripture, rather than instruction by central authority, is the way to faith: at any rate, the effect of Paterson's handling of 'Siesta' is brisker and much more bracing (and in some sense more northern) than Bly's, which seems cushioned and nostalgic in comparison (Bly fares much better in the brief 'Al borde del sendero' – 'Close to the road' – which Paterson renders as 'Tryst'). Something else thrown into clear relief in Paterson's versions is the fact that while Machado treats poetry as an art of community, the poetry of both is often depopulated and solitary, as exemplified in Paterson's version of 'Guadarrama': "Is this you, Guadarrama, the old friend / I'd look for in the blue indifferent eye / of all those lonely evenings in Madrid? / Through your gorges, corries, ragged peaks, / a thousand suns, a thousand Guadarramas / are riding with me to the heart of you."

Here again the natural landscape is used as a guarantor of authenticity by the city-dwelling poet. Such a move would be problematic for many contemporary writers precisely because it would seem *in*authentic, a kind of long weekend of the spirit, glamorized by the requirement to don borrowed pastoral robes. But clearly the journey to the interior as Machado represents it and as Paterson adapts it is at least as much psychic as spatial and geographical. The austere repertoire – road, sky, mountain, sea, river, dawn – is a means of establishing a strangely expansive margin, a stage on which the spirit may enact its search for accommodation and be reconciled to embrace its material limits and its own material nature.

It is no criticism of the richly furnished, thickly textured poetry that characterizes much of the best work of Paterson's contemporaries and immediate elders to observe that its plenitude can seem compensatory, the work of desperation, a warehousing of fragments against a wreck that has already occurred. A currently neglected alternative approach, the minimalist dramatic lyrics of poets associated with *The Review* – Ian Hamilton, some of the early poems of David Harsent, parts of Hugo Williams's *Some Sweet Day* – might have yielded something comparable to Paterson's Machado versions had the poets in question been less resolutely unmystical in temperament. Hamilton himself, cautiously sympathetic to the work of Bly and James Wright, proponents of the 'deep image' in which Hispanic and Anglophone American poetry might merge, characterized Bly's work thus: "His movement has, he says, broken with both 'ideas' and 'things', with the direct statement, with the moral dialogue or parable, with realistic description, with innuendo, irony, anecdote and so on; these are the tools of practical men – they are legs, certainly, but poetry needs wings."[4] Paterson, one might say, is re-making the link between craftsmanly scepticism – his view of poetry is, rightly, wholly practical – and the need to get airborne. In the work up to and including *The Eyes* we witness him growing into his own understanding of what his poetry will necessitate.

For all that, there is something framed and distanced in Paterson's rendering of Machado. It suggests a reaching for imaginative maturity that is still in part an attempt to put theory into practice under experimentally controlled conditions while retaining a sense of deniability, a rope mooring him to the shore, a thread to escape the labyrinth. Perhaps the true test of powers at home with solitude will be intimacy, and this – though by no means largely in a celebratory way – is an important theme of *Landing Light* (2003), a book which seems widely agreed to mark a significant development and an achievement: here, it seems, after the intriguing samples and trailers, is what Paterson, *mezzo del cammin*, can *actually do*.

In 'Waking with Russell', the poem where Dante's famous phrase occurs, the poet embraces maturity through fatherhood, in the presence of a twin son who can be loved for his own sake, not for the reflection he offers/presents to the father, recalling Paterson's version of Machado's 'Moral Proverbs and Folk Songs, 6': "Your Narcissus / begins to fade / as he becomes the glass." There is a clear parallel with Donaghy here in the sense of liberation brought by parenthood, in the presence of another person, new to the world and for a moment immune to it, on whom care can be bestowed (cf. Donaghy's "Don't

---

4. Ian Hamilton, 'The Sixties Press', *A Poetry Chronicle* (1973).

be afraid, old son, it's only me," from 'Haunts'.) But like the succeeding poem, 'The Thread', this is a special case in *Landing Light*. The other poems of love are predominantly about aspects of what Marvell termed love "begotten by despair / upon Impossibility", notably the mismatch between desire and perception, the inability to be for the other what the other perceives, or to be so more than momentarily. 'My Love' formulates the problem exactly: "It's not the lover that we love, but love / itself, love as is nothing, as in O" – the poem opening at the stage where one can imagine many another breathlessly ending. 'A Gift', 'The Wreck' and the retroactive (i.e. post-coital) *carpe diem* poem 'The White Lie' all seem to touch on the same theme. The last of these poems shows a concern for accuracy which the disappointed partner might understandably consider heartless rather than noble:

> [...] one night I looked down
>
> to find the girl look up at me and through
> me with such a radiant wonder, you
> could not read it as a compliment
> and so seek to return it. In the event
>
> I let us both down, failing to display
> more than a halfhearted opacity.
> She turned her face from me, and the light stalled
> between us like a sheet, a door, a wall.

This discomfiting candour is followed by an imperative ("But consider") that Donaghy himself might have employed, which ought to put the reader on her guard. From that point on the seductive nihilism of the argument seeks to win the reader (the partner?) round to the notion that in the erotic life and its probable failure is to be found the only margin of redemption. Amid the massive indifference of the universe of which we happen to be an animated function, we are faced with the task of using consciousness to redeem us from, well, consciousness. In summary it sounds laddish (a bit like the traditional appeal: sleep with me and preserve me from possible homosexuality), but the poem's inequalities of scale give it poignancy too: a Metaphysical poet at work in the seventeenth century might well have adduced the universe to persuade the beloved; the speaker in 'The White Lie' is if anything distracted from the beloved by cosmology (Men! Any excuse!).

   What affinities can be seen here with Paterson's work on Machado? The sense of a godless mystery is certainly present; and much of the time there is an ostensible clarity and directness to the poems, though this arises more from a de-cluttering of syntax and the confidence of the utterance than any actual simplicity of meaning: complex perceptions and proposals are delivered like the plainest sense. The tone is often elevated in comparison with many of the poet's contemporaries. It seems that Paterson has found in Machado not, as Bly seems at some points to have done, a warrant for retiring from the exactions of art towards 'humanity' and 'the natural', but a challenge to be bolder and apparently more direct; at the same time to reject the banal 'realism' of so much contemporary poetry; and to make destabilizing use of fundamental poetic devices such as narrative, allegory and fable alongside complex rhetorical flights: in other words, to be as artful as possible in writing about what might appear to be some very raw emotional material – which presumably comes under the heading of the "inner tensions assuaged in our writing" to which Paterson refers in the 'The Sound of Sense'.[5]

Not for the first time, Paterson and Donaghy seem to have been pursuing parallel enquiries. The first part of Donaghy's 'Discourse on Optics', 'The Heirloom', narrates the removal of a mirror which is losing its silver and becoming transparent. It's left propped up outside "against the skip / So clouds can ghost across the rust. / Though I can't see myself in it, / Still, it's the only mirror that I trust." The only place where the "I" of the poem can be located is *in the poem*, whose suspiciously homely surface reveals a mass of contradictions which can be apprehended but not resolved: how, the poem enquires, could I be more truthful in person than in the complex climate of a poem from which, although I have created its order, I am necessarily absent?

Yeats declared in 'A General Introduction to My Work' that "there is always a phantasmagoria", and that the poet "is never the bundle of accident and incoherence that sits down to breakfast; he has been reborn as an idea, something intended, complete [...] more type than man, more passion than type." Take away the grandiosity, situate the poet in the daily world of getting a living, living with others, taking pleasure and trying to lay hands on experience in order to understand it, and his point remains: the poet is engaged in tasks specific to his or her art, not a version of something else. In a period saturated with anecdotal poems full of appeals to 'humanity', the world as depicted by Paterson and Donaghy must seem strange and often unaccommodating. For one thing they have too much subject matter for

5. 'The Lyric Principle Part I: The Sense of Sound', *Poetry Review*, 97:2.

comfort; for another they take a significant part of their material from areas of human relations for which their intellectual inclinations might seem ill-equipped to some and even, to use a term which has seems (mercifully) to have fallen from use, too 'blokeish'. For the sentimentalist – the enemy these poets are always facing down – nothing is admissible if it falls outside the frame of common consent, and the fact that such consent is itself manufactured somewhere beyond that frame of reference must, according to the common sense of the sentimentalist, mean that it's *neither here nor there* – a phrase containing an unwitting truth, one on which both poets play.

It's tempting to imagine that one of the stimuli behind Paterson's versions of the 'Sonnets to Orpheus' (*Orpheus*, 2006) was impatience with the kind of half-hearted literary grazing that can leave even Rilke sounding like a sentimentalist. We are beset by beautiful feelings. Whose are they? Where do they come from? What do they actually amount to? Having written about Paterson's handling of Rilke elsewhere I don't want to linger here except to point out that in Rilke as in Machado Paterson is drawn to a poet for whom, as for Wordsworth and Coleridge, poetry is an inimitable mode of knowledge.

*Rain* reads like a book that has emerged from a crisis. Its detectable elements include loss (the death of Michael Donaghy), separation and an intensified self-knowledge, though Paterson rarely comes close to writing in a direct confessional mode: torment may fuel the art, but art is the end in view. After the versions of Rilke's sonnets, although sonnets do occur in the new book, there are lots of balladic quatrains and deliberately unshowy couplets, suggesting both the confidence to offer a plainer outline and the necessity of doing so. Formally the work is often noticeably plainer and at some points – such as 'The Lie', 'The Rain at Sea' and 'The Bathysphere' – more peremptory in the introduction of narrative of a kind which brings the poem closer to allegory than to the metaphors to which contemporary readers have grown accustomed and have perhaps come to view as normative.

In 'The Lie', for example, the narrator has for years made a routine of imprisoning The Lie in the cellar. Momentarily distracted, he allows The Lie to speak. It is a blind and bloody child, who asks "*Why do you call me The Lie?*" Having no answer, the narrator gags him again and tries to lock the cellar more securely than ever. The child's question is a fair one: he may be the subject of a lie, but he himself is in fact a truth. Perhaps the force of this strange, powerful, terrible poem arises from the strategy of not revealing what the story behind the secret is: the imprisoned Lie can seem to speak to anyone. It evokes a form of guilt that depends less on the facts of the case than on the knowledge that somewhere they exist, and that by doing so impose a psychic burden or penance that may have as much to do with living at all as with having committed particular acts. If anywhere, the road from this poem seems to lead back to Browning's 'Childe Roland to the Dark Tower Came', perhaps via Anthony Hecht's 'A Hill' and MacNeice's 'Autobiography'.

'The Lie' seems to have a twin in 'The Story of the Blue Flower', which tells of the abduction of a child, recalling the James Bulger case. The poem begins with horrific cinematic realism as the narrator sees his son snatched from a playground: "the two of them / stop his mouth and lift him from the swing / with a kind of goblin-like economy / and hurry off his little flexing torso / to the orange van behind the gate. / And that was that. I knew it was all over."

The narrator descends into the underworld, follows the light of the blue flower back to the surface, discovers his son unharmed and his abductors wandering blinded in the park, crying "like two wee birds". The poem's rhythms are often uncharacteristically flattened, as though to serve as a brake against emotional excess. They also help to situate the poem in the gateway between the everyday daylight world and nightmare. While excluding the word-play which is often an important feature of his work (the exercise of wit would be indulgent and even indecent here, and we recall the leash on which Donaghy keeps it in his own great poem of horror, 'Black Ice and Rain') Paterson delivers us back to an archetypal world where narrative is never far from myth.

The reader who has come this far in Paterson's company will not feel released from literary obligations, however: what kind of poem is this? The critic Graham Hough drew up a clock diagram to describe the range of meaning covered by the term 'allegory'. At noon or midnight he situates 'Naïve Allegory', where theme dominates; at three o'clock 'Incarnation (Shakespeare)', where theme is simple and image complex.[6] Paterson's poem seems to lie between the two, in that difficult-to-hit area of the board. The effect is to reverse the approach of much contemporary poetry, where local verbal effects are used to deliver cumulatively the sense of a generally applicable condition, a world with a train of evidence to support it. 'The Blue Flower' begins at an extreme, with the finished world, from which we try to find our way back to recognizable terrain. It is as though Paterson has found an unexpected passage to ground held in common with Edwin Muir. The Scottishness of Paterson's work – Scottishness in both its visionary and its

---

6. Cited in Richard A. Lanham, *A Handlist of Rhetorical Terms* (1991).

epigrammatic aspects – has clearly grown more emphatic in *Landing Light* and *Rain*. At one time he would not have contemplated writing in Scots like his contemporary W.N.Herbert, but the appeal of Garioch among others has become apparent in a kind of moral pithiness suited to unadorned forms – something held in fruitful tension with a more mystical aspiration.

The blue flower itself could represent many things, besides happening to be a blue flower in the subterranean fields of the poem. Its literary ancestry is traceable to the German Romantic writer Novalis, the subject of Penelope Fitzgerald's strange and compelling novel, *The Blue Flower*, whose betrothed died very young and became associated for him with the blue flower, a symbol so capacious as to represent the aspiration to infinity and possibly its opposite. Yet Paterson is clearly doing more than helping himself to the myth-kitty: the half-mythical terrain of the poem is a scene of terrible avenging violence, seemingly far from Romantic idealism. Although Donaghy at times crossed over into myth (see 'The Tuning', for example), the poem has less affinity with him than with the stern imaginings of Robin Robertson, for whom a poem often functions as somewhere to stage a ritual of loss. Paterson and Robertson both display what Peter Porter has called "the arbitrariness of the genuine imagination", whose starkest examples include Lear's decision to divide his kingdom and Hermione's sixteen-year disappearance from the ruined world of Leontes. Under the same sign there gather numerous fairy tales such as 'Hansel and Gretel' or 'Big Claus and Little Claus' – which are very difficult to read as moralities – and associated German Romantic stories such as Hoffmann's 'The Sandman' and Kleist's 'Michael Kohlhaas'. Given the theatrical connections evident in this list, readers may wonder if Paterson might be inclined to resume his seemingly-abandoned writing for the stage, where 'making sense' can occur at least as much in the event as in the interpretation, where meaning may be 'present', and plainness may be inseparable from mystery.

It would be appealing to conclude on this speculative note, but *Rain* can hardly be set aside without some consideration of 'Phantom', the elegy for Michael Donaghy. The esteem and affection in which Donaghy was held have resulted, in effect, in a series of funeral games in which his colleagues compete to remember and do him justice. Paterson's contribution is preceded by the brief 'Verse': "He's three year deid, an aa I've done is greet / with a toom pen an nae elegy but *och*. / I've jist nae hert to mak a poem o it. / I stole that line from Robert Garioch." The two-way cut of the third line is outdone by the gallows humour of the fourth: to be writing about a silence enforced by loss is still to be writing, by any means necessary, and the implied addressee of the final line would seem to be the subject himself. To write an elegy for Donaghy, then, will involve the scrutiny of what artistic endeavour has meant and amounted to.

The superb authority of the opening section of 'Phantom' – it is breathtakingly concise, the fulfilment of the process of austerity – reads death as an unwriting of life: what remains is a white cup for the anonymous deceased to carry with him beyond Lethe. The cup in question belongs in Roger Mitchell's poem 'The Story of the White Cup', which Donaghy used often in the classroom.[7] The cup, like the blue flower, functions as a symbol at once so inclusive and mysterious as finally to represent the poem's opportunity to exist, its imaginative occasion. This is one of several circles, rings or zeroes to be found in Paterson's recent work (the perfect ring of paint hanging in the jar of water in 'The Circle' is another) and part of its appeal may be traceable to yet another Scots poet, W.S.Graham, in the poem 'Loch Thom', much admired by Paterson: "My mother is dead. My father is dead / And all the trout I used to know / Leaping from their sad rings are dead." It seems to be that kind of simplicity Paterson is after, and part II of 'Phantom' moves towards an ever-starker utterance, past the "white cup" of the saint's hands around the skull which he holds as an aid to meditation, to conclude, with an eerie tonal echo of Graham, "I would say his words are not his words. / I would say the skull is working him."

This seems too bald, and the third section sets to work "to put it otherwise" by scrutinizing a picture by the Scottish artist Alison Watt, in order to complicate things all over again. Is the hole in the piece of material actually 'there', or is it an effect – a "black star at its heart" – to which the folding of the material gives rise? In any case the framing of the picture insists that what is shown is an illusion, while the illusion itself depends on a further layer of falsehood in the "impossible" arrangement of the cloth. It seems as if we are being offered a view from nowhere, a kind of deep-space belvedere from which a glance comprehends a mysterious and implacable unity. Paterson's determination to use poetry as a kind of thinking, rather than be the passive prisoner of period and style and received ideas, recalls *Four Quartets*, in particular the image of divine unity at the close of 'Little Gidding': "When the tongues of flame are infolded / Into the crowned knot of fire / And the fire and the rose are one." In the absence of divinity, in the Rilkean fifth section Paterson nonetheless discerns a fundamental albeit comfortless order:

---

7. *Ploughshares*, spring 1984.

> There is something vast and distant and enthroned
> with which you are one and continuous,
> staring through your mind, staring and staring
> like a black sun, constant, silent, radiant
> with neither love nor hate nor apathy
> as we have no human name for its regard.

All that can really follow this is a key-change, which happens with the introduction of Donaghy's voice in the sixth and seventh sections. The dead man presents a moving target, unwilling to be confined to particular opinions, or to be beatified, or overrated as a musician, or – this is implicit – to approve of the self-aggrandizement to which nihilism is as prone as anything else. If we have been thinking that Donaghy might serve as a Virgilian guide, this is not his intention. The pitch-black rhetorical edifice with which Paterson has – it is suggested – comforted himself, is torn down: "*what kind of twisted ape ends up believing / the rushlight of his little human art / truer than the great sun on his back?*"

The poem closes having given voice to loss but not assuaged it, in a mood of painfully renewed vigilance and mortification, but the defeat is framed and dramatized, made over into art, the very thing the poem has treated as suspect. At this point *Rain* is finished, but not quite over. There has to be a coda. At the very moment when he might seem to be easing up a little, in the title poem which closes the book, Paterson evokes the enchantment he finds in films which begin with rain, an enchantment which survives any subsequent defect of technique or performance. Having taken issue in section V of 'Phantom' with Nietzsche's proposal that the void we stare into will stare back at us, Paterson comes at another famous declaration – "Only as an aesthetic phenomenon is the world justified" – from an unexpected direction: "*forget the ink, the milk, the blood – / all was washed clean with the flood / we rose up from the falling waters / the fallen rain's own sons and daughters // and none of this, none of this matters.*" The rain, it seems, like the white cup, like the circle in the water-jar, is the occasion of the aesthetic, empty of meaning in itself yet charged with inexhaustible possibility, a rebuke, a counsel of despair, a sense of lightness and liberation – whatever it takes.

# Two Tales To Be Telling

JOHN KINSELLA

Michael Donaghy, *Collected Poems*, Picador, £12.99, ISBN 9780330456296;
with references to *The Shape of the Dance: Essays Interviews and Digressions*,
Picador, £12.99, ISBN 9780330456289

The finest poems in this landmark book are the final ones of *Safest*, that would have been part of Donaghy's next collection had his brilliance not been cut short. Not just confronting death but giving us, his readers, a way of coping with our own mortality – surely the greatest gift a poet can offer – these are all masterpieces, innovative, and characteristically technically astute. I will come to them in due time.

I need to state from the beginning that maybe I don't view Donaghy's poetry in the light by which it is usually seen. This is not to say that I contest Sean O'Brien's scrupulous, sensitive, and intelligent introduction to this book – in fact, I most often agree with him or find myself wanting to write things he has already said, or, at least to reaffirm his observations – but that I perceive Donaghy as *more* than a revitaliser of a formalist tradition. As O'Brien puts it: "For those who cared to notice, Donaghy was among other things renovating some features of the scholarly, formalist American poetry of the 1950s and 60s, whose leading exponents were Richard Wilbur, Anthony Hecht and James Merrill."

Indeed, Donaghy's work shares many points of contact with these fine poets; but in the end, despite his American (Irish) origins, Donaghy's poetic sensibilities seem to owe more to his adopted country than to where he comes from. Yes, John Donne is there, and one might argue that almost-vivacious smart first volume, *Shibboleth*, is metaphysical in design, but present too are William Empson, W.H. Auden (in his pre-American phase), and even the Australian 'expat', Peter Porter. In interview, Donaghy discussed conditions of reception and his consciousness of the way that both British and American reciprocal investments of style and voice can dominate critical response. For example, he "held back" the 'O'Ryan's Belt' sequence of poems until after the publication of his first book (it forms part two of his second, *Errata*), because "I knew that once I broached the matter of Irishness or Irish folk music I'd be typecast as 'the Irish American musician poet.'" Donaghy was equally concerned with interpretations of his Bronx "proletarian" background and other imagined qualifiers of a poetics. This poet knew how he *didn't* want to be interpreted as much as how he *did*.

*A propos* his background, Donaghy also mentions the prevalence of knives (used by neighbourhood gangs) in his childhood: which offers an additional way of looking at the various references to blades and sharpness throughout the work. It's a line that's often drawn along life, love, and death and fate: 'Occam's Razor'. Donaghy mentions Hopkins and Dylan Thomas as poetic influences (both are easy to see), and also Pound. I wonder about this. Maybe the Pound of 'Hugh Selwyn Mauberley' or *Cathay*, but not much the Pound of the *Cantos*, as I am sure Donaghy himself would have agreed. Having said this, the late unresolved fragment 'Irish Folk Music' might stylistically owe something to the *Pisan Cantos*.

Despite this discussion, in the end I'd have to argue that, however fascinating such contextual reading might be, it's not fruitful to try and approach Donaghy's work – of all poets' – through his influences. All poets have these, and some wear them more obviously than others, but Donaghy is his own measured and hyper-controlled 'self'. There is nothing arbitrary about a Donaghy poem, even if his thematics embrace arbitrariness and chance itself. The poem is an icon, but no icon is to be trusted.

Donaghy's almost larrikin wit; his ability for paradoxical self-denigration while producing something seriously concerned with the self; his ability to make the commonplace, the incidental, or even the literary, resonate well beyond their moment, are characteristic of so much of this *Collected*. Donaghy plays with formalist conventions but doesn't elevate them as things in themselves. This might seem peculiar given the deep craft involved in every clause, every line, every stanza. These are possibly, along with work by O'Brien himself, the most honed poems being published in English. But they are not chipped out of stone; they are engagements (often playful) with language itself.

Donaghy views ideas and literary ideology as fair targets, and does not hesitate to ironise his own art. Literary history is about coteries and tastes, national and personal politics, as much as any intrinsic value. But to ironise modes of reading is not to denigrate sources or a literature. For example, in his 'hoax' poem sequence, 'Seven Poems from the Welsh', irony plays against the 'othering' of a literature for the sake of fetish consumer value, while at the same time deeply respecting craft and sensibilities of pastiched 'originals'. Donaghy is a metatextual poet, for whom form is not the shaper of poem, of meaning, but a trigger for challenging content. Irony, wordplay, deployment of 'pop culture' icons working in literary and philosophical contexts ('high art'), allow Donaghy to create an environment where a greater seriousness is possible because no claim to a privileged position as 'all-seeing' poet is established. What is established is an absolute certainty of control, so that we trust the links, the juxtapositions, while the play is going on. This pairing of trust and irony creates a unique tone: I know none quite like Donaghy's. He invites us to go with him and we inevitably accept.

One of the failings of much contemporary reviewing, aside from the like/dislike, or good/bad, binaries, is that a reviewer will look to the obviously best poems to serve as an illustration of a poet's skill. I think one learns most about a poet's abilities from a 'lesser' or seemingly 'minor' poem. Take, for example, 'A Disaster' from *Shibboleth*. Here's the poem in full:

> We were ships in the night.
> We thought her rockets were fireworks.
>
> Our radio was out, and we didn't know
> The band was only playing to calm the passengers.
>
> Christ, she was lovely all lit up,
> Like a little diamond necklace!
>
> Try to understand. Out here in the dark
> We thought we were missing the time of our loves.
>
> We could almost smell her perfume.
> And she went down in sight of us.

One need not labour the obvious irony of a ship sinking while observers think it's celebrating some mysterious occasion. Nor need we linger over the conceit of the ship as woman, the objectification and fetishisation of the female body and the suggestions of surface (sexual) enjoyment and internal distress and suffering. Irony sustains these aspects almost nonchalantly, and in a way that leaves the reader as much accused of insensitivity and lack of astuteness as the poem's observers. That's a characteristic rhetorical device, with Donaghy implicating and sharing complicity in failing with the reader. We identify with the persona/e's flaws as if they are our own, and certainly those of broader social responses. In his longer poems (never too long – a full page or just over is a longer poem for Donaghy), this technique is used with great rhetorical complexity, and with many diversions and crisscrossing of irony and tone that are inevitably brought together at the end of the poem, not by way of 'closure', but sometimes with tragic overtones. It's why his approaching-death poems are so powerful and necessary beyond their obvious personal import.

But back to this short piece. What lifts it out of the 'matter-of-fact' is the fourth couplet. The pithy, aphoristic accumulation of the previous lines, with their relatively light deployment of the figurative, is undone here. The caesura between "understand" and "Out" necessarily couples and bridges the darkness of the personae and the inevitable experiential darkness of the reader (doubly ironic because of the clarity of the poem). "Out here" is also "in there" and "in you" and "in us". One of the most rewarding aspects of Donaghy's work is how non-excluding it is. To use a cliché, he wears his learning lightly; but it's more than that, it's a political choice not to allow language to hoodwink the reader. Don't get me wrong: his poems are often imagistically complex, image frequently working simultaneously with a series of rhetorical devices, but their aim is not to delude or show themselves as superior. Learning serves a function, and that function is to share knowledge of the fragility, and its attendant ironies, of the 'human condition'. To return to that couplet: the second line is as much sad reflection as an ironic augmentation of the poem's main drive. It works both ways. As in the final couplet, the objectification of the sinking boat as "she" is entangled in the genuine issue of attraction. It's a poem built out of paradox, and this operates like a key to unpick the Donaghy of many poems: including, in the first volume, the disturbing 'Auto da Fe' and 'Ramon Fernandez'.

Donaghy's second collection, *Errata*, is a different book altogether, though it maintains the tones and techniques developed in his first. Let's pause for a moment and reflect on Donaghy's constant assertion, in interviews and elsewhere, that the measure of a poem for him was always aural, and that the mnemonic links between traditional musical 'forms' and the form of a poem (he was known to compare the 'reel' with the 'sonnet' in this context) were fundamental to him as a poet: not mere formal truism, but also part of content itself. It has long bemused me that while a negator of the 'postmodern', Donaghy was in many ways one of its richest exemplars. True, he opposed the façad-ism of post-modernity (which he rightly located in its architectural origins), and deeply rejected the faddism of a self-perpetuating 'avant-gardism'; but in his appropriations, plays, and linguistic inventiveness, he shares as much in common with say, Ashbery, whom he very early on imitated and later rejected, as with the Dylan Thomas who caught his ear as a child.

Donaghy was right to reject the promotional aspects of any movement or cluster that defined itself to the exclusion of other practice, but in some ways I think he found himself in a position of having to stand up for a position he didn't textually hold. He himself said that a poet like Olson, whose worth he entirely rejected, influenced him as much as a poet he admired, by helping him understand what it was he *didn't* want to do in poetry. Negative influence is as valid as 'positive'. This picture is complex. In the same way – rejecting syllable count as an artificial mode of constructing a poem, and favouring the 'beat' as more natural, and more to do with the building blocks of poetry – Donaghy actually undercuts his own dexterity when it comes to making poems. He utilises 'beat' and 'syllabics' in most of his work; a contrapuntal effect between these overlapping modes of constructing the line is evident in many poems, especially those where pastiche forms the dynamic. Donaghy was incredibly astute at articulating what his position wasn't, but I am not convinced he actually fully realised how much of a 'link' his work forms between formalist and 'postmodern' poetics.

If Donaghy was slightly bemused at why *Shibboleth* received so much acclaim, and his stronger follow-up *Errata* less, then the answer to that puzzle might well be found in the hybrid nature of this masterwork. The poems that make up the second section of *Errata*, 'O'Ryan's Belt', are as good as any he ever wrote; and as a larger work, if we might interpret this group of poems as such, his most vital to my mind. As it shifts between 'places' (Manhattan, the Bronx, Chicago...), the notion of heritage (Ireland, but not exclusively) invests the 'folk' with immediacy and necessity: music and consequently poetry become a marker of identity and purpose. Donaghy shifts between narration and idiom with ease, and, ironically, with the deftness of a prose master such as Joyce. Maybe this is not so ironic, as Donaghy himself once noted that his influences came as much from the rhythms of prose writers (such as Defoe) as from poets. What Donaghy manages, as well as anyone writing in English has ever managed, are shifts in mode and voice within a single short poem. This is the skill of a realist novelist merged with the mythic and folkloric resonance of a Yeats:

> When Anne Quinn got hold of it back in Kilrush,
> she took her fiddle to her shoulder
> and cranked the new Horn of Plenty
> Victrola over and over and over,
> and scratched along until she had it right
> or until her father shouted
>
> > 'We'll have *no* more
> > Of *that* tune
> > In *this* house tonight.'

She slipped out back and strapped the contraption
to the parcel rack and rode her bike
to a far field, by moonlight.

It skips. The penny I used for ballast slips.
O'Ryan's fiddle pops, and hiccoughs
back to this, back to this, back to this:

The long quote shows these effortless shifts in tone and temporality. It's more than a tense change; it's more than going from scene-setting to explication (from 'show' to 'tell'), and it's more than moving from a more expansive to a more compressed line: it's a movement in and out of aurality. It is interesting to compare the musical phrasing of the line "Victrola over and over and over", with its slight variation on the word "Victrola" and then relaxation into the easy memorability of trochees that comes with the narration, to the line "back to this, back to this, back to this:". The latter is easily memorised with its repetition of phrase and anapest, but the switch in mnemonics marks the shift in narration (point of view, tense, and so on). It is always worth bearing in mind that Donaghy recited his poems from memory at readings, and that they were seemingly built out of the compilation of recitable elements. This might well account for the fluidity in shifts and slippages of 'modes', even within very short poems.

Not everything we do is anchored in the 'aural', and though for Donaghy the measure of the poem was aural, he recognised that there were other modes. In his famous essay 'The Shape of the Dance', he says of the marks left on a Chicago dance floor by the dancers' shoes after the evening's entertainment was over: "This pattern, I recognised, was an enormous encoded page of poetry, a kind of manuscript, or, more properly, a *pediscript*." And though he said he didn't write concrete poetry, Donaghy certainly registered the representational. A metonymy of sign and sound infuses the writing. It is easy to forget that he also wrote a lot of poems about the 'visual' (ways of seeing), and that sound and sight are ultimately inseparable in his work. Interestingly, the poem that precedes the 'O'Ryan's Belt' 'sequence' is entitled 'A Discourse in Optics', in which, in *part i*, an ironic metaphysics of self-reflection, heritage and absence/loss ('heirloom'), plays against pathetic fallacy – "That full-length antique bevelled mirror / Wants to be clear water in a trough" – to become a discourse on the lyrical self and paradox of the failure of that self and its reassertion (grounded by the heirloom's destiny, a rubbish skip):

I'll prop it up outside against the skip
So clouds can ghost across the rust.
Though I can't see myself in it,
Still, it's the only mirror that I trust.

In *part ii*, 'The Pond', the posture of 'nature' is inverted, with a pond providing the reflection, but the same questions, regarding the self and the characteristics of subjectivity, are explored. Here, nature becomes the manufactured object – the reverse fetish:

Except those times light strikes the basin level
And almost makes a window of the surface
To show our shadow amid coins and gravel
Outgazing the sad overcoat and face

The 'emotive' aspects of these 'epiphanies' are rendered 'neutral' by the precision of the language and form.

The social dynamics of the 'O'Ryan's Belt' poems; the implications of musical and poetic form for law and order ('Patrolman Jack O'Ryan, violin' and Police Chief Francis O'Neill); and the folkloric as a vehicle for gritty realism as well as repository and preservative for community identity and narratives: these are aspects of this small group of poems that need exploring at length (as I hope to do in a future essay). A poet who refuted nationalist agendas, rejected political and social posturings, and was deeply embarrassed by being labelled a 'New Generation Poet', Donaghy struggles with the myth of the self when set against national and cultural backdrops. I am constantly brought back to the disjunction between the architectural perfection of the poems as artefacts, and their deeply troubled sense of 'self'. The 'I' was Donaghy's anathema, as it is for any thinking poet. The Language poets he so reviled were, Donaghy felt, caught in the paradox of their literary production and yet self-declaration as authors: but this was also his struggle.

Rather than make general comments about Donaghy's third, highly accomplished, collection *Conjure*, or the selection of uncollected poems that conclude the book, I'd like to use the rest of this essay to look at a few of the last poems in his unpublished final collection *Safest*.

Wordsworth's 'Composed Upon Westminster Bridge' anthropomorphises the city of London as living flesh, and bestows an agency on the entire corpus while noting the autonomy of parts, its limbs. In Donaghy's sonnet 'The River Glideth Of His Own Sweet Will', a younger self filled with the prospect of the living city confronts the dying/vulnerable self wired to the (heart) machine of the city. (Machines have a particular disturbance as symbol and actuality for the poet.) This poem, gleaming with clarity and gentle irony, becomes both self-obituary and a declaration of love for place that echoes against futility. It normalises and almost sanctifies the futility of the regular, the expected, the mundane: "What unaided eyes could possibly connect / thirty years across Westminster bridge / through traffic fumes, crowds, / children, career, marriage, mortgage?" The poem's beauty and depth is in its simplicity.

'Exile's End' speaks across the phases of dying. The poem is the poet's epitaph, and its 'voice' removes itself from the context of body. In fact, this notion of dialogue of soul and self runs through Donaghy's work. The poem becomes the flesh, the embodiment, but it is *not* the poet. The poem begins with a semi-naval metaphor, a world of fluid and violence that's undercut by the rush of vulnerability: "Wait then for a noise in the chest, / between depth charge and gong, / like the seadoors slamming on the car deck." One image is filmic and imagined, the other familiar. Naval and civilian collude and offset. As the poem progresses, the ordinary and matter-of-fact ("a nurse's bald patch") merge or 'blur' with the past. The body is alienated from the 'self' through death, but the voice of the poem continues in its metaphysics: "Turn away. We commend you to the light, / Where all reliable accounts conclude." The end is affirmation. Darkness is not the end: light is.

The final poem of *Safest*, 'Two Spells for Sleeping', is incantation, invocation, and farewell. These spells for sleeping are for the dying and for those left behind, a loved one in particular. A hermetic love poem, 'Two Spells' also resonates like a folk song, an affirmation to be passed on through the generations. It is personal and communal, local and universal, like all great songs and all necessary spells. From this tough, intellectual, and gritty poet, a gentle but robust leave-taking:

> In the soft dark welling,
> two tales to be telling,
> one spell for sleeping,
> one for kissing,
> for a leaving.

# Gwyneth Lewis
## *from* A Hospital Odyssey

### *Book 9*

*Coming is real. Going is real. What you do*
*in between is a game.*
                                    – Ĕṟṟāpragada

*The present moment is a powerful goddess.*
                                    – Goethe


Have you ever wished that you could stop time,
and examine the world while it's perfectly still,
picking its pockets? The metre's ticking and I'm
stuck on the Underworld. I could steal
from translations of Dante and spend a while

doing the devil and Virgil, "Abandon all Hope",
but you've read that already in other books.
I even devised a more modern trope.
The entrance is check-in, Charon's the bloke
who drives the dead, who are travelling folk,

to the airport, where the baggage carousel
is out of order. You get the idea:
flights are cancelled, all the hotels
are booked. Demons are terrorists wielding fire,
the damned have no papers and diarrhoea.

Very contemporary, very timely,
the runway's closed, due to fire or ice.
But this won't do because it's fancy.
R.S. Thomas – I can hear his voice –
told me once that I should choose

between fancy and imagination.
I know it's the latter that I revere,
so the hell-as-an-airport idea is gone,
but I may well use it later.
Now I'm taking the risk of not being clever.

This is the Otherworld. It isn't hell.
I'm no Orpheus, plucking the usual lyre,
it's a Celtic *Annwfn* and I'm a cell.
The note I'm seeking is the DNA
of talk. My body's the paper

on which life writes. Like music and film,
poetry excels at close-up and slow-motion,
it alters how we see space and time,
makes us their masters by changing their signs
for a while. This is why art is medicine

of kinds, although I'd take the chemo
as well as iambic tetrameter,
if I were ill enough and had to.
One thing's sure, a poet's no doctor,
but part of what a good life's for

is reaching outside of your own body.
This can mean partners and children, but some
take up residence in the city
of words and make a hospitable home
from wider linguistic chromosomes.

There's no such thing as a single bee
in nature or, if there is, it quickly dies.
The greatest achievement of humanity
is language and this is the body to which I've
made my commitment, to the hive

of speaking. In this poem's cosmology,
my Otherworld is a place to one side,
not higher or lower. Reader, will you grant me
your breath? Because I may have died
by the time you read this, and I need a ride

in your mind. It's only for a little while.
Think of yourself as scuba gear,
state-of-the-art, of course, because style
means stamina. No, there's little danger,
if I can work out where to go from here.

*

They found themselves on a barren strand.
A great wind buffeting the shore,
so violent they could barely stand.
It was as if a demented creature
was flinging itself, found everywhere

unbearable. They spotted a pier
and moved towards it gingerly.
"I don't see any Underworld here,
do you?" asked Maris. Out in the bay
the wind was raising wisps of spray

like ghosts who turned in tormented eddies
then died back to water, sinking like sand
in a dusty desert. It appeared the sea
was burning. "I don't understand
this weather," said Maris, leaving solid land

to walk the jetty, feeling brave,
inching over the lively water.
Beneath her the jostling chaotic waves
made her giddy. "This atmospheric pressure's
weird," said Ludlow. Savage cats' paws

teased the currents. "I suppose being ill
is this unstable." Uncanny fog
sank towards them down a barren hill.
With it came the smell of crags,
sundew rotting in clammy bogs.

It settled like the creamy head
on a pint of Guinness. The air grew dank,
touched them so eerily that they edged
out on the pier, and instinctively shrank
from the all-annihilating blank.

But out in the offing, the buffeting wind
raged ever harder and a water spout
took shape and began to wind
its way towards them, its transitional throat
moaning with force. It finally smote

their platform and, with a roar
caught them up inside its maelstrom,
whirling them, pell-mell into thin air
then, ears popping, it spiralled them down
into the waves. There is a skin

of mind-altering, exquisite suffering
between life and death, just like the surface
of the sea, the shock when entering
the airless prairies of the abyss.
The companions fell together, weightless

as corpses. Their blood was singing,
lungs bursting but soon they found
they could breathe, just as the dying
are deep-sea creatures being drowned
in the thin atmosphere of land.

Like stranded dolphins, we keep them moist
with dampened towels and blankets until
the weight of oxygen in a labouring chest
is impossible and they find they have gills
for another medium. Or like a seal

wife whose drenching night-time sweats
show where home is. Morning reveals
her outline in salt on marital sheets.
She leaves at last for the joy of neutral
buoyancy, the supported fall

into the Otherworld beneath the waves.
Maris watched the grains of sand
like gold in the water. She gave
Wilson a look. "Don't leave me behind,"
she thought. He answered, "I understand,

I hear you speaking." "That's odd," she thought.
"Not really, you and I are one,
it's easy for us to communicate,
I'm part of your internal conversation."
"What about Ludlow?" "Medical man."

They grabbed him. He gave *Thumbs up* and
                                                all three
sank from the tumult into new ease,
their bodies adjusting to weaker gravity
and instinctively, they moved with grace
into deep water and timelessness.

They landed softly near a shipwreck.
Maris listened to her own breathing.
They waited and, slowly, through the murk
they saw a shoal of shadows approaching,
not the dead but those half living,

even on land they carry a weight –
fathoms of water. "These are depressives,"
said Wilson, "they live without light."
"But how can these people be only half
dead?" "How can you not be, if you're fully
                                                alive?"

retorted Wilson. Maris stretched out her hand
to a man unable to smile or speak,
but her natural gesture was overwhelmed
by internal refractions. She missed his cheek
and watched a human being sink,

then he was swept by colder currents
to somewhere darker. The friends explored
the shipwreck. There, figures leaned
exhausted on a rocks, bits of broken propeller.
"These people have forms of dementia,

a crime against time. Nobody minds
a toddler's amnesia, we find it funny,
the endless repeating of nursery rhymes
can be charming. Not so that infancy
in geriatrics. Keeping company

is all we can do as parents regress
into forgetting who their children are,
what food is for, or how to dress.
This is death with the living. And over there,"
Wilson gestured, "are treatments for cancer."

Maris made her way to a sunken van
with fish in its windscreen, bright as cartoons.
Patients were waiting. Each one had been stung
by the asp of a blood test. In hospital gowns,
they looked like initiates. "Is Hardy among

this monastic order?" Maris searched
but couldn't find him with a bald head
from chemo. Yet others were scorched
by radiotherapy, where they willingly died
in parts of themselves, so they could survive

for partners, children. A white-haired woman
darted towards them. "That's Marie Curie,"
said Wilson. "Discovered radium."
A swimmer in life, she was fully at ease
underwater. She requested news

of her work. "I hear that the gamma knife
is much more effective, a precision tool
compared to radium that took my life
but earned me fame and my Nobel.
Does that which killed me, make others well?

No, my dear, don't get too close.
I'm radioactive. Polonium burns
me still, not even the ocean can cool
the heat of nuclear decomposition
that powers everything." She turned

and glided away, on a thermocline
of interest only to the dead.
"She's always been my heroine"
said Maris. The companions drifted
deeper and noticed that the seabed

was sloping downwards towards the gloom
of steely waters. Natural light
turned metallic and a plankton bloom
made seeing difficult. Ludlow cried out
when gloaming parted and they caught sight

of a soldier emerging from a cloud of gas,
wearing a mask like the head of an ant.
He stopped, looked round and revealed his face.
"Who are you?" asked Maris. "I'm Sergeant
Ludlow," he sighed. "Is this the Salient?

Oh no, I'm forgetting. It's quite elsewhere.
This isn't Ypres, I recall, and I am dead.
It takes us all some time to recover
from dying, though why I should return to this
                                              field
I don't know. I was injured here, not killed,

joined by war to the larger body
of men who've mixed their flesh with mud
in battlefields everywhere. I'll never be free
of that wound, it will forever link my blood
to richer harvests round Mametz Wood."

"You were very daring to join the gas corps,"
Maris, surprised, heard Ludlow say.
"Not really, I didn't know enough to fear
the wind in those pre-mustard gas days."
"They use it now in cancer therapy,"

said Dr Ludlow, "an internal Somme
at cellular level, and so it's saved
hundreds of thousands who've overcome
malignancy and have achieved
the truce of remission." "Grandson, you still live.

I've learned the body's greater than the soul,
if briefer. It's not true that desire
ends with dying. What would I not give to feel
my skin raised to goose-bumps by evening air?
Or to smell the roots of your mother's hair

as I used to daily? Now I have no tale,
no narrative, no transformation,
nor work to do. I'm restless, volatile,
a member of that rootless nation,
the dead, whose endless mass migrations

wear me to nothing." The soldier wept,
exhausted by the eternal sorrow
of the disembodied. And then he slept
and slowly he and his pack were swallowed
into the ooze that means no tomorrow.

They wandered into a gloomy reef,
Wilson went ahead but turned, aghast
at what he saw. With inconsolable grief
he howled. From the depths the massed
canine dead began to file past.

They all moved slowly and emerged
made large by water – legions of dogs enlisted
                                              to fight
in wars not their own. Some were messengers
in trenches, many were shot
with their owners. Then those who submitted

to vivisection. Bosun, Lord Byron's
dog. Those who pulled the sleds
in the Antarctic. Then the silent thousands
of greyhounds disposed of when they grew too
old
to race, butchered with a bolt to the head.

Laika, the mongrel who died in orbit,
Belka, Strelka and Little Bee,
stifled, then burnt to small meteorites,
Mushka, Damka – Little Lady –
all run with Sirius now. The dogs that died

saving their owners from water or ice.
A terrier torn apart by pit-bulls,
defending his children. Dogs that had no choice
but starve, the ones who were faithful
beyond all reason, waiting outside a hospital

for dying owners. Wilson cried.
You think a dog's unable to shed tears?
You're wrong, I've seen it, in the eyes
of a spaniel whose leg was caught in wire
until we freed her. Saddened and sobered,

they swam down further into water's grain
to a deep-sea smoker, where volcanic heat
stripped out everything but a strain
of basic bacteria. In abyssal night
misshapen fish spoke out in light:

eat or be eaten, fluorescent displays,
life-forms as delicate as lace
but harder than diamond. Here sky weighs
like death. Wilson eased his pace
and said solemnly, "Now we're at the place

where things that never lived are seen.
Some say they're myths and chimeras.
The human mind, as you know, is a screen
onto which we project many wonders
and, if we're lucky we might see her."

"Who?" "Helen of Troy." "She didn't exist,"
said Ludlow. "Wasn't she an eidolon?
Doctor Faustus lost his soul for a kiss
from Helen, a daemonic vision.
She was an idea. No flesh-and-blood woman

could have caused such madness." "She was
virtual,
an image of such attractive youth
her presence demolished all other ideals.
Beauty's no more than transcendent health,
symmetric features, a sign of wealth

in the genome. Helen, nevertheless, is real.
The camera sees her in James Dean, Monroe –
fleeting glimpses – no individual
can bear her for long. Violence follows
her footsteps." "Tell her to show

herself," said Maris. "I want to see
the form of perfection that Paris chose,
the eyes that made it worth razing Troy.
I want to see the glory we all lose,
though we never possessed it." They scanned
the shadows.

Nothing. An underwater breeze
made them shiver. Then a dynamic shimmer
silvered the water. An electric charge
thrilled through Ludlow, made Maris quiver.
It was a feeling like spring fever,

the excitement of making fierce love.
It was something like the scent of new-mown
            grass,
it was a delirium. Maris felt herself alive
like a comb of cells with surplus
sweetness, dripping with rapturous

honey. And suddenly the black
was burnished, filled with a pulse
which, to the ear of her ear, came back
like the faintest music of sensuous dances,
such as the wild extravagance

that moves kelp forests with the hiss
of everything tearing but then made whole
by its own movement, which is bliss.
Maris felt wholly viable
vigorous, fresh and pliable

as corn in a field, which you can hear grow
on summer nights, if you care to listen.
Maris sat down, overcome with joy
and, in the mud, saw something glisten.
She reached out her hand. A ring with a stone,

black diamond set with flaming opals.
It slipped on her finger like a promise,
a blessing, a ritual, a formal betrothal
to new life made in dust and detritus.
As Helen of Troy, the goddess passed

in brightness so keen that it was cruel,
you'd give your life for a brief affair
with such smarting. Merely feeling well
was nothing compared to being this aware.
You could die for her and she wouldn't care

or save you. Maris heard: "Love isn't enough
to rescue anyone. You need the principles
beneath everything." Then the goddess left.
The three ascended, tracking the bubbles
of breath and found an anchor cable

leading above them to the bobbing cloud
of an awaiting neat black curragh.
Wilson stationed himself at the prow
and the boat made weigh, though nobody
            steered
or thought to talk to one another.

They sailed a long time. The travellers stared
for hours at the water and saw the places
they knew in their youth and were hypnotised
by thousands of dear and indifferent faces,
crushed by the waves' incoming staircases.

Maris looked down at herself. The world went
            through
her body, as if she were made of smoke or mist.
They could see horizon through her tissues.
Her body was porous, nor could she resist
the tiniest fluctuations of light,

and now she found that even pain
went through her, with the weather.
Life showered her like shimmering rain.
It was dusk and Maris could no longer
            remember
the colour of Hardy's eyes, his features,

but that didn't stop her pressing on,
even though she'd lost his gravely voice,
it didn't matter. She hummed a song
about sailing without chart or compass
and soon they saw the Island of the Blessed.

# Jonathan Barker

## WENDY COPE

I first met Jonathan in the 1970s. He was working in the Arts Council Poetry Library, which was then housed in Covent Garden. I was a London teacher and had recently developed a serious interest in poetry. The Library was a wonderful discovery. On Saturdays I would go in to change my books. Jonathan was always willing to have a chat about what I'd been reading, and to make recommendations. I appreciated this greatly because at that time I didn't know anyone else who would talk with me about poetry. I have felt a special affection for Jonathan ever since. When my poems began to be published he was encouraging about them and I'm grateful for that too.

A few years ago I was asked to judge the poetry section of the Whitbread prize. The organisers didn't want more than one poet on the panel. They asked me to recommend people who were knowledgeable about poetry but were not themselves published poets. Jonathan was the first person who came to mind. My other suggestion was the journalist and radio presenter Tom Sutcliffe. Our day together was the best judges' meeting I've ever attended – calm, amicable and immensely interesting.

In 2006 Jonathan rang me and asked if I would like to take part in the 2007 Walberberg Seminar outside Berlin. I wasn't too sure about this at first, as it meant reading to an audience of German academics. I imagined a roomful of very serious Herr Doktors and Frau Professors. But when Jonathan said he would be there too, I decided it would be all right. It turned out to be tremendous fun. The German academics were delightful people and they laughed at my jokes. After the reading, I was interviewed by Jonathan, who is, of course, superbly well qualified to interview just about any contemporary poet. It gave me great pleasure to be interviewed, more than thirty years later, by the person who had been so kind and helpful when I was just beginning to write.

Wendy Cope's tribute to Jonathan Barker was written for the occasion of his retirement from the Literature Department of the British Council, where he was the valued ally and honorary agent of poets for many years.

# CRITICAL VIEWS

Gold in the blood,
Everything you know.
— *Jane Draycott*

# The Man Question

JANE HOLLAND

Hugo Williams, *West End Final*, Faber, £9.99, ISBN 9780571245932;
Fred Voss, *Hammers and Hearts of the Gods*, Bloodaxe, £8.95,
ISBN 978185224846

Reading Hugo Williams's poems is akin to being presented with a plate of very expensive, exquisitely-made petits fours. Spoilt for choice, you don't know which to pick, which to recommend. There is no particular complexity in the writing, but the flashes of brilliance are in the detail, where William's clear-cut observations arrive, understated – "the beard / showing up like iron filings underneath the skin" – or force the reader, as all good poetry does, to see things from a new perspective: "I draw up the sides of my mouth / in the signal for pleasure."

A keynote in this latest offering from Williams, a T.S. Eliot award-winning poet whose last collection was *Dear Room* in 2006, is memoir. This consists for the most part of schoolboy anecdotes: some a little slapstick, some downright disturbing. Here we find the ritual humiliations of youth, *sangfroid* under pressure, and a gradual slide toward the more adult pleasures that form the other key ingredient of *West End Final*: a fascination with women, their wiles and poses, their tricks and intrigues.

Amongst these schoolboy poems, the bluff, almost cartoonish note of 'A Suitable Cane', describing

> the knobbly 'School' cane,
> the curve-handled 'Pop' cane,
> the straight but bendy 'House' cane,

is offset by the uncomfortable possibility that this anecdote, the humorous tale of purchasing a cane and having it used on the buyer, is based, at least in part, on real memories of childhood canings:

> The whirr of air, the sudden punctuation mark.
> And then the absorption, the storing away
> of anything like tears or cries,
> as if for later use.

The ability of poets to store away their experiences, real or imaginary, 'for later use', funds many of Williams's nostalgic pieces and portraits, some so skilfully drawn that they become almost visual. The most significant of these are the two sequences: one for the poet's mother, and the other titled simply 'A Pillow Book', its twelve poems numbered rather than named. This has been framed as a repetitive, circular narrative featuring the beloved in various bedtime poses – *demaquillage* in the dressing-table mirror, the act of disrobing, getting into bed – which deepens in emotional impact as it winds in on itself, lending delicacy and a certain pathos to the finale of this book:

> I should collect these things
> to remember you by.
>
> Each one pauses for a moment
> to imprint itself on the air,
> before slowly detaching itself
> and disappearing forever.

Undemanding, whimsical, often drily humorous ("He could light his own cigarette, / but he needed a man, he said, / to look after his lighter"), these poems would do much to enliven a dull train journey, and are short enough – Hugo Williams considers it a failing if a poem 'goes over the page' – to be popped into the mouth between stations and allowed to dissolve slowly. Be warned though: they may fizz.

One of the few things US factory worker-cum-poet Fred Voss shares with Hugo Williams is that his poetry provides 'easy reading'; it does not indulge in obscure wordplay, nor juggle the telling metaphors of a mainstream lyric. Fred Voss hammers out poems in a terse, plain, largely unpunctuated language, part of that American tradition where confessional meets colloquial. His latest collection, titled *Hammers and Hearts of the Gods*, calls to mind the mighty Thor, or perhaps the comic strip *Asterix the Gaul*, all those larger-than-life characters of a more heroic age. Except this is very much a book of the *now*, albeit a present which has been mythologised in places.

Voss is not unaware of the shortcomings of this style, nor of his own unorthodox background, as the fiercely-named 'Only Poets with Clean Hands Win Prizes' demonstrates. Consequently, perhaps, he bolsters his work with frequent references to other poets, from wild-man Bukowski – with whom it is clear he closely identifies – to earlier Romantics like Shelley and Coleridge: "Bukowski waited to die / in New Orleans and I turned the pages of books / with fingers blackened by the filthy skin of steel bars / and Coleridge gave lectures / instead of finishing *Kubla Khan*". Many of his poems focus on male conflict, both internal and external. One of Voss's regular characters, the taciturn Frank, has to nurse his beloved wife through a terrifying illness, compared to which he finds "2-ton steel mill drop hammers / [...] easier" to handle. War plays a key role in this collection too, with Voss finding himself making gun barrels, bomb bay door handles and "hand rails / for attack helicopters". Rather too frequently circling back to the shame he feels over victims of the Iraqi conflict, Voss cites the need for steel workers to earn a living, whilst admitting, in a poem about army parachutists, that:

> Sometimes we get more than we bargained for
> when we open our toolbox
> in some shop
>
> Sometimes we are jumping down out of a door
> into Hell.

Yet Voss finds this noisy, Dantesque environment, where "I have seen men go to every extreme they can / to prove / they are still / human", a source of inspiration. There is tenderness here, and moments of relief from the endless machismo; even Frank briefly relaxes his tough inarticulacy in the company of his wife. One such tale of male bonding comes in 'Peace Conference', where a potentially dangerous, racially-inflamed exchange with a young Mexican on the shop floor ends in an awkward *entente* between the two workers:

> and he sticks out his fist
> toward me and I stick out my fist
> toward him and we knock
> knock our fists together...

To convey the peculiar violence and emotional inadequacy of factory existence, Fred Voss has adopted something similar to the "super-simple [...] super-ugly language" developed by Ted Hughes for *Crow*. It suits his candour and feels natural enough, though when Voss moves away from the factory it is no longer as ideal. Nonetheless, his latest collection provides another excellent record of a life rarely, if ever, documented by a poet from the inside.

Jane Holland edits *Horizon Review*; her latest collection is *Camper Van Blues* from Salt Publishing.

# Each Singing What Belongs To Him

TARA BERGIN

W.D.Snodgrass, *Not for Specialists: New and Selected Poems*,
The Waywiser Press, £10.99, ISBN 9781904130352;
Stanley Moss, *Rejoicing: New and Collected Poems*, Anvil,
£14.95, ISBN 9780856464171;
Wyatt Prunty, *The Lover's Guide to Trapping*, The John Hopkins University
Press, £12.50, ISBN 9780801892790 / 0801892791

At a reading in Atlanta in May 2008, W.D. Snodgrass – who died in January 2009 – introduced himself as an 'unconfessional' poet. He was removing himself from the category into which he had been placed fifty years ago by M.L. Rosenthal, in his article 'Poetry as Confession'. Snodgrass explained: "One, I am an atheist; two, I'm not writing some bedroom memoir; three, I'm not saying I've done anything wrong." Although he rejected the term 'confessional', *Not for Specialists: New and Selected Poems* serves as an important illustration of Snodgrass's place in the development of self-revelatory poetry.

Postwar guilt and the loss of his daughter through divorce caused the poet's breakdown, gave him writer's block and led him to psychoanalysis. But these things also became the subjects of his most famous poems, 'Heart's Needle' and 'After Experience Taught Me...', the writing of which became part of his recovery. The poems remain vivid, especially 'After Experience Taught Me...' in which Snodgrass punctuates a lesson from his combat instructor, who taught him how to blind and then kill a man with his bare hands, with words from the philosopher Spinoza. In his *New Poems*, Snodgrass returns to military imagery, but it is his heart, "poor drummer", that must now march in time ('Pacemaker'). These new poems also continue to speak in a very personal voice, and the book closes with a tender, final 'Invitation' to the poet's wife. In 1960, Snodgrass won the Pulitzer Prize for *Heart's Needle*, but as he recalls, it cost Louis Untermeyer his job as Pulitzer judge: the poems were considered too private. Snodgrass went on to receive many awards and honours but remained wary, admitting: "I am not particularly pointed toward winning." His poetry's success probably lay in such an attitude, and this selection illustrates how he repeatedly defended his approach to poetry, insisting: "There is a loveliness exists, / Preserves us, not for specialists" ('April Inventory').

Another substantial publication from America this year is *Rejoicing: New and Collected Poems* by Stanley Moss. By choosing to arrange the book in reverse chronological order, Stanley Moss has done what John Cheever once wished he could: "It would please me," wrote Cheever in 1978, "if the order in which these stories are published had been reversed and if I appeared first as an elderly man [...]." For Moss, the decision works very well, because his most recent poem becomes the opening and title poem 'Rejoicing', a title that captures what is central to this book. In it, the speaker swims in a sea that is both God and God's womb; God is "wilderness" and "cold" but also happiness and freedom, "without commandments". Such a merging of God and man into the femaleness of nature recalls not only Whitman (with whom Moss begins his poem 'Subway Token' about September 11), but also the English poet Ted Hughes. In another poem, 'Listening to Water,' Moss directly references Hughes's 'How Water Began to Play,' responding to Hughes's lines "Water wanted to live / It went to the sun it came weeping back", with the much more positive: "Water wanted to live. / It went to the sun, / came back laughing."

Moss is editor and publisher of Sheep Meadow Press, a non-profit press with a special focus on international poets, and his involvement with translation is very interesting, because this volume highlights his celebration of, and ability with, language: in particular his ability to return a given word to its literal origin while at the same time making it new and revelatory to the reader. He does this expertly again and again, for example in 'El Sol', 'Peace', or the difficult, emotional poem 'The Miscarriage'. Lawrence said that Whitman was the first to destroy the moral conception that the soul is superior to the flesh. Stanley Moss continues his tradition in a collection that shows a poet who delights in the elements of things:

> The man who never prays
> accepts that the wheat field in summer
> kneels in prayer when the wind blows across it   ('The Blanket')

Wyatt Prunty's new collection *The Lover's Guide to Trapping* is a slimmer volume, but no less valuable. The poems, which strike a fascinating balance between simplicity and intricacy, are as Prunty says in the long poem 'Parks', "sometimes easy, sometimes not". They deal with simple subjects (a mole, a man, a childhood memory), but do so with lines that often play out in an unexpected, complex way, appearing unfinished yet proving on re-reading to contain a carefully crafted meaning. In 'Circus', stillness is "the last remove":

> Deeper than landscape and untouched
> By any hand, poised counterweight
> And unexpended force, the botched
> Arc of the final acrobat

The book opens with a mole tunnelling through the rich dark earth, making patterns like letters. Surfacing, the mole is "Quizzical as the flashbulb blind". This marks a recurring theme with Prunty: a journey made through darkness into light, driven by the "unnamed will". In 'Lincoln's Tunnel', one of the more obviously autobiographical pieces, the poet sits in a cab, stuck in traffic in the tunnel under the Hudson. First remembering his own youth by the rivers of the South, the poem ends with the cars moving up into the daylight: "Outward now, as from the mystery of intent / To be the mystery of an unnamed will, / As light is blindness in the afterflash / Of waiting for the light to come again."

Prunty presents the core significance of his subject-matter in a subtle way, so that the reader comes upon it slowly and with satisfaction. Perhaps the best example of this is the final poem, 'An Early Guide to Trapping', which by a simple trick of titles, nudges us towards understanding his point. Because of this, and his gentle but skilful use of rhythm and rhyme, Prunty is like his 'House Wren': "It was a small, plain bird," he writes in that poem, "I heard it sing two things at once."

Tara Bergin is studying for the PhD on Ted Hughes's translation of János Pilinsky. She has published poetry in *Poetry Review*, *Poetry London* and *Modern Poetry in Translation*.

# Poetry Is Not Innocent

ASTRID VAN BAALEN

Mahmoud Darwish, trans. Catherine Cobham, *A River Dies of Thirst*,
Saqi Books, £10.99, ISBN 9780863566349;
Nicole Brossard, various translators, ed. Louise H. Forsyth,
*Mobility of Light, The Poetry of Nicole Brossard*,
Wilfrid Laurier University Press, £9.99, ISBN 9781554580477;
Valérie Rouzeau, trans. Susan Wicks, *Cold Spring in Winter*,
Arc, £9.99, ISBN 9781904614302/3

Edward Said said of Mahmoud Darwish's poems that they "transform the lyrics of loss into the indefinitely postponed drama of return." *A River Dies of Thirst* contains the posthumously published poems, salvaged, as Ruth Padel poignantly describes in her Preface, after the Israeli army ransacked Darwish's office in Ramallah in 2002. Clearly having abandoned the constraints of form in favour of predominantly prose meditations, this is writing in which aesthetics and ethics lock arms in sharply arresting imagery, where we find "a girl laughing and crying / in the far corner of the poem", and Darwish put "in front of the television to witness the rest of my death with millions of other viewers." The postponed drama of return indeed. The short, sharp shock of the solitary figure despairing at the impotence of "the heroism of the metaphor" in 'Beyond Identification' unavoidably shadows the poems that follow, where this very "drama of return" propels the wry wit and lyrical intensity of alterity:

> Even if you were not the dazzling presence you are:
> I would be the absence in you that I am – inside and out.
> Your presence is translucent, crystalline.     ('Most and Least')

These meditations lay bare a choreography of thought on how to write and breathe a life of poetry in the safe-haven that turned out to be Darwish's true homeland: language, "a refuge in my image of you and I / in you of me" ('Private Meeting'). The inter-shifting masks of presence/absence dominate throughout to break in the final aphoristic poem, 'You are You', falling in step with his heavily politicised life of exile one last time: "I cross a broad street to the wall of my old prison and say: 'Greetings, my first teacher in the laws of freedom. You were right: poetry is not innocent!"

Definitely not innocent is the erotically charged poetry of Nicole Brossard. Although she's not using the ode metre, the sapphic theatrics of corporeality steam off the page, "June aroused by audacity / precise lips or this allurement of the clitoris / its unrecorded thought giving the body back / intelligence" ('(4):Lovhers/Write'). Ellipses, parataxis and reification ripple through her poems at a controlled, physically perceptible pace, suggesting a surgical treatment of her material: "skin / hesitating between philosophies and the dawn" ('between history framed in visions'). Thought gets sutured to shifting imagery and semantic registers, such as for example in 'a way of flopping on the bed' where "the light made our thoughts so supple we could taste the / embrace and weather, alter bodies and selves."

Brossard's poems often work best when read as sequences (*Lovhers* and *Typhon* spring to mind) and even though Louise H. Forsyth's selection provides the reader with an insightful overview, the mechanics of coherence that characterise individual collections are rather over-determining in *Mobility of Light*. A second difficulty I found is that even though the translations are accurate and carefully drawn, successfully engineering both poetic structure and meaning, the erotic *va-va-voom* of the French is at times missing in the English. Take for instance the evocative "*vous et moi tout en sueur*", where "*tout*" swallows "*vous*" like an act of acoustic, feminised fellatio: "you and I all in sweat," ('Muscle's Law') just didn't quite do it for me.

Having said that, *Mobility of Light* pulls together the work of one of that rare breed of poets who keep reminding us that (I quote Brossard quoting René Daumal): "Prose speaks about something, poetry does something through words." Brossard herself writes in her afterword that *Mobility of Light* is "in contrast with a biography, my bio-semiology." Spanning four decades, it offers a sweeping retrospective of Brossard's poetry from 1965 to 2003. And not before time, as this formidable doyen of feminist formalism has certainly left her mark on a tradition of poets who explore thought-as-body-as-text, or *cortext* as Brossard would have it, a

> result of getting short of brea   th's
> the x of ex      axis of pleasure

Just over two-thirds of the way into *Cold Spring in Winter*,

> The sky's up on its pedals, dancing.
> Sometimes the sun right in your eyes

> I take my father's bike.
> Radiant with spokes as if set free

and as the poem goes round and round "always spoking freely", I'm convinced that (a) I am reading a weird and wonderful book and (b) the translation is a laudable achievement.

*Cold Spring in Winter* is French poet Valérie Rouzeau's debut collection. It came out in France in 2003. It's a lament for the death of her father, who ran a scrap yard: a pertinent fact as it is simply quite dazzling to witness how Rouzeau mimics his job of picking through scraps of glass, metal and paper with her own delving into language's backyard of puns, inversions, slangy neologisms and fragments of songs and sayings:

> Not deadying oh not desperish father
> everlast get up run fast –

and later:

> My father my father my father on earth
> as he is in summer wind in winter wind.

Through linguistic and semantic games of hide-and-seek with her childhood self, Rouzeau chases memories of her father with the urgency of her fear that they might become unremembered. To achieve and sustain this effect of "babble and squeak", Rouzeau has edited *in* rather than *out* the baby-talk of elision, pot-luck "gerundation" and meaning driven by sound and speech patterns that children tend to pick up on intuitively, when for example her father's voice drowns "the goats' as walking baaack you feeling baaad / saying secret tiny words of tenderness."

If the reader starts wondering how this goat could have sounded so good in the original (*"balaaade toi malaaade"*), it's a sure sign of a good translation. The French lyrical tradition of Rimbaud and Baudelaire has been in the freezer since WW1 (for decades now to write a lyrical poem is to commit a *faux pas* in most literary circles in France), in favour of experimentalism and word games. Wicks has understood this and, give or take a couple of safe bets, she has resisted the temptation to cover any quirkiness with a lyrical muffler and has quite brilliantly saved a poetic technique from being lost in translation. As Wicks says in her translator's preface, she took a gamble and it paid off. As for Rouzeau, this poet has found a truly authentic voice in what will doubtlessly be a glittering career this side of the Channel.

Astrid van Baalen is a poet and translator and a co-founder of the Pars Foundation. She is currently completing her first book of poems.

# What Lodges In One

DAVID MORLEY

Samuel Menashe, *New and Selected Poems*, with DVD *Life is Immense* by Pamela Robertson-Pearce, Bloodaxe, £12, ISBN 9781852248406; Anise Koltz, trans. Anne-Marie Glasheen, *At the Edge of the Night*, Arc, £12.99, ISBN 9781904886600; Jane Draycott, *Over*, Carcanet, £9.95, ISBN 9781903039922

"I never thought it was a poem. I thought it was just [Menashe slides arm slowly downwards] a sigh". This is Samuel Menashe speaking in the film *Life is Immense: Visiting Samuel Menashe*, by Pamela Robertson-Pearce, which comes packaged with his *New and Selected*. Menashe writes concisely. It's rare in a review to be able to quote in full but with Menashe we have open season. Here are two untitled poems that give the sigh of pure brevity:

> The sea staves
> Concave waves.

and:

> A pot poured out
> Fulfils its spout.

Ian Hamilton Finlay wrote that, "I feel more and more that the purest poetry exists in single words or seemingly minute effects. These are what lodge in one" (from Thomas A. Clark's suitably spare edition of Finlay's letters, *A Model of Order*). For Menashe, purity of diction requires a purity of contraction:

```
The niche narrows
Hones one thin
Until his bones
Disclose him.              ('The Niche')
```

*Eleven words. Fourteen syllables.* This is writing about which Donald Davie once commented, "[Menashe's] poems have to be compact and close because only in that way can English words – *any* English word, if the right tight context be found for it – show up as worshipful, as having a wisdom and an emotional force beyond what we can bring out of it when we make it serve our usual occasions". As Menashe might have said, *Less is more as God is love.* (Menashe would probably contract this to *Less is love.*) Reading this excellent selection, you can't help but admire Samuel Menashe's integrity of perception, his self-possessed seriousness, and the precise, often playful awareness of the importance of space – as another means for stating, imparting and whispering.

Menashe's restrained epiphanies come over strongly in performance. I met this fine poet at the Ledbury Poetry Festival last year. His resonant, gentlemanly, measured delivery woke rich meanings and sounds from the stringed air of each poem. This is what a Slow Poetry should sound like: honed not only in drafting but in delivery. It helps to hear the poet, and it is a pleasure to watch him articulate his working methods and aesthetics. The film of Menashe reading his poems in his tiny New York apartment is a welcome extra and shows fine moments of generosity and insight. Any open-minded reader of poetry will warm to this man and this book.

Anise Koltz, Luxemburg's best-known poet, is similarly scrupulous about brevity. *At the Edge of Night* brings together four recent collections. Koltz originally wrote in German but, in a move characteristic of her trilingual country, has crossed the linguistic frontier into French. She believes that "when a Germanic sensibility is transfused into a Latin language, something almost physical takes place – the transfusion produces a kind of spark".

The world of Koltz's poems is austere, un-indulgent and un-indulged. The poems certainly 'spark', but what that flash of language leaves on the mind resembles an after-effect against a blackout:

```
Life is no long quiet river
but a bloodbath
```

Yet you ask me for
poetry decorated with flowers
with little birds

I'm sorry Ladies and Gentlemen
each of my poems
buries your dead                    ('Prologue')

I need to contextualise my own critical response by saying that I was probably reading Koltz at the wrong time in my life. I may have been searching for longer moments of light among the wire-drawn darkness of her poetry. Her austerity is in its way beguiling and inviting. At one point she writes, "Because this poem is a lie / it has the right to be beautiful". But the fictive "I" in Koltz's poetry never seems too far from a reality that is battered by grief. Her husband's death in 1971 as "a late victim of the Nazi occupation" gives rise to the brief emotionally-riven poems of *Fire-Eater*:

When my love was born
I washed him
with my right hand

When my love died
I washed him
with my left hand

Without a future
I stay behind
both hands severed

Jane Draycott's last collection *The Night Tree* (2004) was an exceptional book. At the time I celebrated her patient intelligence of practice, and concision of address, not only in every poem in that book but in the very philosophy of perception informing her poetics. I believe she has ground in common with Samuel Menashe. Like him, she has the wisdom to leave things out; she has a gift for the music and tone of a poem; and she won't be rushed into betraying her vocation through lack of care or pursuit of fashion.

*Over* is an acutely musical book. Sean O'Brien was right to praise it recently for its "quietness": it is quietly mesmerizing. Its sequence of twenty-six poems based on the International Phonetic Alphabet sounds at first like an Oulipian exercise. But the music of Draycott's language allows the poems to exceed and escape their framing, becoming something quite other than the sum and sound of its sections:

> A match struck
> in the house of ice.
>
> Deep-sea flame fish
> calling, the heart
>
> harpooning. Something
> in the dark is flashing.
>
> Gold in the blood,
> everything you know.
>
> The fire on the little sandy beach.
> The bear at the window.
>
> No one escapes.                    ('Whiskey')

For me, though, the clinching moment in this admirable collection is the extract from Draycott's translation of the medieval dream-vision *Pearl*. The language is marvellously modulated yet stirringly wild. Draycott has carried over into our tamer, tired world a strong, strange sense of how original, gorgeous and natural this old poem can be. I look forward to the complete translation if the extract is anything by which to judge it:

> And I saw that the little hill where she fell
> was a shaded place showered with spices:
> pink gillyflower, ginger and purple gromwell
> powdered with peonies scattered like stars.
> But more than their loveliness to the eye,
> the sweetest fragrance seemed to float
> in the air there also. I know beyond doubt
> that's where she lay. My spotless pearl.

David Morley has published two new pamphlets: the Templar Poetry Prize winner *The Rose of the Moon*, and a limited edition *The Night of the Day* from Nine Arches Press. His next collection from Carcanet is *Enchantment* (2010).

# Encounter And Witness

ALEX SMITH

Charles Tomlinson, *New Collected Poems*, Carcanet, £25,
ISBN 9781903039946;
Vuyelwa Carlin, *The Solitary*, Seren, £7.99, ISBN 9781854114709

Among those who value Charles Tomlinson's work, it is something of a commonplace that a new reader should be directed to 'Swimming Chenango Lake', one of the great poems of the twentieth-century. But in truth, a newcomer to Tomlinson's work can make a start anywhere in the *New Collected Poems*. There has been no diminution in the quality of his poetry over the decades. His latest work is as keen and fresh as that in the earlier volumes, and the range and variety of forms employed continue to surprise and delight.

It is just over fifty years since Charles Tomlinson's first full volume of poems, *Seeing is Believing*, appeared: published, significantly, in New York (it was another two years before OUP published it in the UK). Writing about Tomlinson's volume *Skywriting* in the *Guardian* in 2004, David Morley, referring to poets and critics outside the UK, said "you may be knocked for six to learn that for them English poetry is a triangular constellation made up of Charles Tomlinson, Geoffrey Hill and Roy Fisher." Not much has changed; "neglect breeds neglect" as Morley says. The long neglect of Charles Tomlinson, surely one of our finest poets since the war, is extraordinary.

Tomlinson is an 'Edenic' poet in the sense that he delights in exploring the world's phenomena; in poem after poem, the reader is invited to encounter the world afresh. Interviewed by William Cookson, Tomlinson characterised his work as "a phenomenological poetry, with roots in Wordsworth and in Ruskin."[1] Objects and phenomena are accorded their own rights, as things to be observed rather than used as an extension of the self. This is at one with Tomlinson's renunciation of extremity (always the trap of solipsism):

> Scriabin, Blok, men of extremes,
> > History treads out the music of your dreams
> Through blood, and cannot close like this

---

1. *Contemporary Poets*, 3rd ed., ed. James Vinson, St Martin's Press (New York)1980, p.1544.

> In the perfection of anabasis. It stops. The trees
> Continue raining though the rain has ceased
> In a cooled world of incessant codas [...]  ('Prometheus')

One could analyse in depth the skill and consummate craft that have gone into the making of this, and so many other poems. What Tomlinson's poetry notably lacks, however, are the overriding claims of personality.

Tomlinson was always an internationalist and appreciative of Modernist techniques: which did little to enhance his reputation among narrow literary coteries in England. After working and travelling in Italy in the 50s, he travelled to America where he met William Carlos Williams, Marianne Moore and George Oppen among others. Tomlinson combined his interest in Augustan and early Romantic verse (Pope, Johnson, Coleridge, Wordsworth) with that of the American poets (Stevens, Moore, Carlos Williams, Oppen, etc.) and the result often employed a shortened line, but kept the traditional cadences of English verse alive through rhyme (often internal) and finely balanced accents, as in this passage from 'Reflection':

> A reflection on the pane
> has repositioned the chest of drawers
> under the mahonia bush
> on the lawn outside.
> One drawer lies open to the rain
> perfectly dry. Let the eye
> follow that image
> to where an interior door
> cuts across the night,
> as if there were many mansions to explore
> under the gathered gloom [...]

Nothing from Tomlinson's seventeen volumes published by OUP and Carcanet has been omitted here, so we are now able to see for ourselves what a superb achievement the *New Collected Poems* represents; one which no one with an avowed interest in poetry should be without. This is a volume to treasure for a lifetime.

Good poems depend in part for their effect on the constructed spaces within them, on what is *not* said, on the economy of the writing. This is superbly demonstrated in *The Solitary*, Vuyelwa Carlin's fourth collection. Throughout the volume, which is in four sections, Carlin's creative intelligence is at work making use of those spaces, fine-tuning each line. These qualities manifest themselves immediately in the opening poems which portray her grandchild, Magdalena:

> You have known, already, dreams: some bad;
> your new sorrows stir old constructs –
> arc into future-shock [...]

Every word is considered; there is no slippage, no cop-out easy cliché. There are occasional echoes – for this reader, for instance, of David Harsent in 'Dead Child with a Bible' – but this can be seen as a coincidence of reading, not influence: Carlin's voice is very much her own.

The first section observes two young grandchildren and an autistic son. The second is a series of sensitive portraits of elderly people suffering from dementia, while the third deals with South Africa, where Carlin was born, and wartime Poland. The final section is a sonnet sequence which searchingly explores the religious life. Re-reading the volume I was struck by a number of images: "atom-clusters", "stardust, moving and shaking", "irradiation of the body" and "yet you roar in the firmament" and was reminded of Marlowe's "strong line" in *Doctor Faustus*; sure enough, in 'Tudor', one of the poems dealing with people suffering from dementia, we come across a direct quotation: "See, see, where you, and Christ, stream / through nerve-clinker; the firmament", so I take this as a kind of thematic thread. These poems are gentle and tender and far from being exploitative (the poet worked for five years with older people with mental health problems). Meanwhile the section dealing with wartime Poland would need a lengthy appraisal to do it justice, but I believe that not since Carol Rumens's 'Outside Osweicim' have we seen such work of arresting power.

Alex Smith has just put together his fourth volume of poems.

# ONE THAT GOT AWAY
# Passionate Attention

DOUGLAS HOUSTON

Sarah Maguire, *The Pomegranates of Kandahar*, Chatto & Windus,
£9.00, ISBN 9780701181314

Sarah Maguire's rich lyricism is inseparable from the neutrally factual tone with which her poems accumulate detail to shape powerfully felt and imagined worlds. Her objectivity frequently adopts a scientific precision in the treatment of the botanical and geological elements which are at the heart of much of her best writing. 'A Fistful of Formaminifera', for example, builds its wide-ranging image-structures without deviating for a moment from facts of natural process and microscopic observation:

> Benthic,
> their galaxies carpet the depths of oceans [...]
>
> They conjure their houses
> from flotsam and jetsam
>
> tucking grains closely,
> between alveoli

The way these lines unobtrusively pass along the rhythmic pulse that propels them is characteristic of Maguire's poetry.

The spare fluidity of her stanzas infuses the scrupulous economies of Maguire's imagery with constantly varying dimensions of musical interest. 'The Physic Garden' sequence offers good examples of serendipitous sureness of ear. It traces the progress of four seasons through minute attention to the lives of the flora:

> Disease infuses
> the garden's roses
> as a fungus pools
> around the stilled blooms.

The intimacy of response Maguire brings to her numerous horticultural close-ups is continuous with her deep attunement to the earth and its processes on a global-ecological scale. Poems set in the Middle East, Africa, Europe, and USA give geographical substance to the world view that emerges in her work. International politics are equally a factor in the humane registrations of suffering and dispossession that are conveyed in the sharply focused detail of such poems as 'Ramallah':

> a provisional city
> a concatenation
>
> of loose roundabouts
> building sites
> and razor wire –
> scars of forced demolition

'The Sand Fulmar' offers a fine example of the range and integration of the human and geological perspectives that open in the poems. The opening view of a dredger on the Thames expands to take in the interactions of exploitative industrial purpose and the natural cycles of drainage and renewal at "the slow hearts of rivers":

> soft migrant grains
>
> will bed down in darkness,
> a promiscuous mingling
>
> of mica and silica,
> of small bones and smashed shells,
>
> of beach glass and rock quartz,
> with sandworms,
>
> with seaweeds
> torn up from their roots.

Waterways are presences throughout the book. The Thames, the Nile, the Neva, the Seine, the Jordan, and the canals of the Low Countries bring the life and movement of water to the planetary frame of reference the poems outline.

*Pomegranates*'s numerous low-key love poems are of a piece with the rest of the collection in taking imaginative form from observed natural phenomena:

> For one hour at midsummer the sun climbs higher than these walls.
> And here I am, indoors, in darkness, walled in by sorrow and ink.
>
> The moon is doubled in the Nile, reflected in the Thames.
> But look up at her: bone-cold, alone [...]                  ('Reflection')

Maguire's poetry has very much to recommend it. Its sustained openness holds the attention and rewards it with consistently high levels of interest and pleasure.

Douglas Houston is a writer and editor living in Huddersfield. His *New and Selected Poems* is due to appear in 2010.

# Angels In The Architecture

MARTYN CRUCEFIX

Margaret Atwood, *The Door*, Virago, £9.99, ISBN 9781844084586;
Billy Collins, *Ballistics*, Picador, £8.99, ISBN 9780330464383;
Rita Dove, *Sonata Mulattica*, Norton, £16.99, ISBN 9780393070088.

Atwood first came to prominence as a poet, and *The Door* is no mere by-product of her acclaimed career in another genre. Possessing great architectural coherence, it can be read as an extended sequence, the first and final parts dealing with personal topics while the middle sections consider the role of the artist. The autobiographical poems range across childhood, old age, the death of Atwood's father and the slow decline of her mother, "like watching somebody drown" ('My Mother Dwindles...'). Atwood writes magisterially on topics that form the bedrock of much contemporary verse, and she concludes with the title poem, which employs simple language and repetition to trace a lifetime of responses to the "door" of mortality – moving from fear, dismissal, puzzlement, to a final reconciliation with the "god of hinges" who has eerily "kept faith".

Elsewhere, Atwood's colloquial voice, deployed through mostly short-lined free verse, urgently debates poetics: we might "pick over the language" or "poke sticks" into our brain or pursue something "more [...] group-oriented" ('Possible Activities'). At times, art plays a consolatory "sugary old hymn" as the Titanic sinks ('Boat Song'); at others the poet declares for more of a Cassandra role: "That's what I do: / I tell dark stories" ('Another Visit to the Oracle'). Most often, artists suffer neglect, as in 'The Poets Hang On', where they stand with "begging bowls" as voices sneer "Cripes, they're pretentious". This is no straw argument, but a wrestling with the worth of a life devoted to words.

If politics is the fraught narrative played out between power and its victims, then Atwood declares injustice and suffering are as inevitable as the weather "thickening itself / with sand and body parts and broken / chairs" ('The Weather'). She re-evaluates the idealism of the Sixties in 'White Cotton T-shirt', and the futility of a retreat to Nature in 'Bear Lament'. She creates iconic or mythic figures to articulate her views; and her sympathy for 'The Last Rational Man' suggests she sees her role as similarly admonitory and unheeded. Yet she has powerfully topical things to say, especially about defeat which "is never in the past". The victorious soon forget, but defeat is long-lived, it "soaks into the present / [...] It bursts into song. / Long songs, you understand". ('Nobody Cares Who Wins').

Promoting political engagement, Atwood teases more anodyne writers: "No deferential smiling, no baking of cookies, / no *I'm a nice person really*" ('The Poet Has Come Back…'). It's hard not to pigeonhole Billy Collins as just such an inoffensive, obliging artist: his work charms, disarms and sells well. Reading him is like being accompanied by an articulate, ironic, modest, fallible, puzzled, curious companion. When so many poets present themselves with some 'street' credibility, Collins is refreshingly seen checking his dictionary, brewing tea or simply lighting "three candles / and [...] pouring myself a glass of wine"('Quiet'). His reflective voice following the meanders of thought in precise, elegant and startlingly transparent language. *Ballistics* is full of confident addresses to his readers, as in 'August in Paris', where he wonders where we are while he makes notes for the poem. But there is none of Atwood's sense that artists work unregarded: Collins discovers his reader "where there is only the sound of your breathing / and every so often, the turning of a page".

And turn the page we do. There's a destabilising, ludic quality to Collins's self-referentiality that suggests a none-too-taxing postmodernism as we stand within and without. 'Brightly Colored Boats Upturned on the Banks of the Charles' opens, "What is there to say about them / that has not been said in the title?" What also makes Collins's work enjoyable is his imaginative gift, as when he conjures a "four-moon planet" and lovers on a beach mistakenly believing they experience closeness as "he gaze[s] at one moon and she another" ('The Four-Moon Planet'). Such poignancy is dissolved, diffused and re-created, as Coleridge argued imaginative creation must. There are fewer such moments in *Ballistics* than in earlier collections, but many of these poems leave the reader up-lifted and sensitised to the beauty of the world. Who else might call a poem 'Despair', lamenting "gloom and doubt", only to recommend the ancient Chinese poet "Wa-Hoo, whose delight in the smallest things / could hardly be restrained, / and [...] his joyous counterpart in the western provinces, Ye-Hah".

A similar exuberance in *Sonata Mulattica* confirms how far Rita Dove has come from her early, restrained austerity. Across two hundred immensely readable pages, she traces the life of George Bridgetower, born in 1780 to a Caribbean/African father and a Polish/German mother. A brilliant violinist, Bridgetower travelled Europe, rising to such prominence that he premiered a Beethoven sonata originally dedicated to him. However, the two men fell out over a woman and the piece was re-dedicated to Rudolphe Kreutzer, who considered it unplayable.

Bridgetower's rise and fall is narrated with terrific gusto in a plethora of voices. Although scattered with the unthinking racism of the time – and Bridgetower's origins identify him as one of those displaced figures Dove has always been drawn to – the sequence reads more as an exploration of the thrills and pitfalls of celebrity. Plucked from relative obscurity by Haydn, who "reaches down to cup / the rough head, murmurs: / *There's music in here*" ('Friedrich Augustus Bridgetower Discovers the Purposes of Fatherhood'), the boy makes his debut in Paris at the age of nine and is soon performing in theatres as the "pathological hit of the day: nigger on a golden chain" ('Black Pearl').

Dove encompasses a mind-boggling range of form and conjures the period without becoming bookish or parodic. She evokes the beauty of Bridgetower's playing – drawing "a fingerwidth of ache upon the air" ('The Performer') – and Beethoven's composition – "this sobbing / in the midst of triumphal chords, / such ambrosial anguish" ('Polgreen, Sight-Reading'). The portrait of the composer is done, with wonderful economy, as a man who "cannot stop listening" ('Ludwig van Beethoven's Return to Vienna'), a "squat invasionary force" ('First Contact'). But Dove is more interested in

Bridgetower's slow decline. His eventual death in Peckham, London, is witnessed by an ignorant neighbour who is "afraid he'd sprinkle / some of that brown my way" ('The Witness'). Norton's blurb calls the book "grandiose yet melancholy", but the impression it really leaves is of a vibrant world, populated by extraordinary characters, as capable of mean and selfish action as they are uplifted and redeemed by their art.

Martyn Crucefix's new collection, *Hurt*, will be appearing from Enitharmon in Autumn 2010.

# Translating The Personal

### ANTHONY CALESHU

Radu Andreiscu, Iustin Panţa, Cristian Popescu, *Memory Glyphs*,
trans. Adam Sorkin, Twisted Spoon Press, £7.90, ISBN 9788086264325;
Trevor Joyce, *Courts of Air and Earth*, Shearsman, £8.95, ISBN 9780907562955;
Leanne O'Sullivan, *Cailleach, The Hag of Beara*, Bloodaxe,
£7.95, ISBN 9781852248185;
Laurie Duggan, *Crab and Winkle*, Shearsman, £10.95, ISBN 9781848610491;
Giles Goodland, *What the Things Sang*, Shearsman, £8.95, ISBN 9781848610545;
Lisa Dart, *The Linguistics of Light*, Salt, £12.99, ISBN 9781844714452;
Mark Halliday, *Keep This Forever*, Tupelo Press, £10.29, ISBN 9781932195729.

Of the seven books I'm reviewing here, the two most engaging are translations. The first, *Memory Glyphs* translated by Adam Sorkin, brings together three prose poets well-known in Romania but little (if at all) known in English: Radu Andriescu, Iustin Panţa and Cristian Popescu. Sorkin's fine preface is valuable for its clear attention to the intersection between each author's oeuvre and their biographies, which it soon becomes clear forms a significant part of the poetics of at least two poets. Referring to himself in the third person, Popescu's poems perpetuate a personal mythology that transcends individual experience as he explores his relationship to family, religion, and death. Panţa's work isn't as concerned with the autobiographic, but still exploits a personal 'I' in poems of love and lust, often made by juxtaposing the trivial (a wrong number dialled, sour cherries from a tree) with the serious. Popescu and Panţa both died in their mid-thirties (in 1995 and 2001, respectively) but their work, with its willingness to move between the real and the imagined world, has successfully "retrieved personal autobiography" (as Sorkin writes) for Romanian poetry.

Radu Andriescu is of the same generation, but his poems are more concerned with texturing almost generic experience with language. Poems rush through an abundance of observation and thoughts, layering detail upon detail:

> soon enough... the sun rises... the terrace, the table, the plastic chairs... the towers of Galata Monastery, the red satin fez forgotten at the street corner, the little satin shoe lost under the chestnuts and oaks at Negruzzi High School, the telephone line dead, the doors closed, the apple tree withered, choked with vines... the filing cabinet stuffed with names... an apocalyptic Bucharest, a kind of Iasi, post– ...

The reader gets to fill in the gap: *post-communist, post-modern, post-surreal*.

Trevor Joyce's *Courts of Air and Earth* brings together his excellent translations from Middle and Early-Modern Irish. All these poems are elegiac, full of remorse and lamenting past lovers or lives lived. *Buile Suibhne* has a long history of being translated, and Joyce's 'The Poems of Sweeny, Peregrine' (first published in 1976) is a major re-telling of the story of the king who is cursed in battle and turned into a bird. As Joyce is one of Ireland's better-known poets of the avant-garde, it's not surprising that these "experiments in translation" are wonderful reinvigorations of the originals. 'Love Songs from a Dead Tongue', a sequence of eighteen poems (brought together for the first time), is written in the persona of the tenth century queen Gormlaith and, as throughout, Joyce's ability to grieve in another's voice makes for a moving performance. The relationship between elegy and love poetry is further clarified in two 'Anonymous Love Songs from the Irish', while the one previously unpublished poem, 'Séan O'Duibhir of the Glen', reveals Joyce's ability to convey the true sorrow of the 'outcast' as he makes myth, or, in this case, a folksong, modern:

> Fox red on rock keeps lookout
> on the horsemen's hurly-burly
> and the woman by the wayside
>     lamenting scattered geese.

Like Joyce's book, Leann O'Sullivan's *Cailleach, The Hag of Beara*, takes its voice and subject from Irish myth. There's no doubting O'Sullivan's impressive ability to capture the Cailleach's note of longing (for love and touch) and remorse (of a lover died and the Cailleach's loss of human quality as she reverts back to the stone from which she came). This is O'Sullivan's second book, and it's an ambitious undertaking which in places really sings with metaphor and image:

> I kiss and break open,
> until he starts to moan, grass-sweet drippings
> of his mouth, as though he's making me a gift
> in the quiet before each breath, guiding my tongue
> back along the path none but another animal could follow.

The greatest reservation I have is that these poems rarely deviate in tone. It's tough to ask a book to be cohesive and then to fault it for repetition, but one wishes... in my case, as finely wrought as these poems are, I wished for less *wrought* and more variety of form, experience, and sentiment.

*Keep this Forever* is Mark Halliday's fifth collection. Halliday is also a well-known critic and reviewer of poetry, and this book dramatises a life spent thinking about poetry. The first section is dedicated to the subject of his father's death and early establishes the self-awareness which pervades the book as a whole. There's very much the wish here not to be "sheerly stupidly ordinary", as he writes in one poem; but it's one thing to be self-aware, another to let the reader know that you're self-aware, and still another to let the reader know that you know that the reader knows you're self-aware. By the time we get to 'Cloud of Luck', with its parenthetical last stanza beginning "(Note to self: omit this one. / Too vulnrbl – why give such easy ammo to hostile reviewers?)" I'm wishing that the poet would leave his knowing (if consistently self-deprecating) self out a bit more so that we might get a chance to enjoy some of the fine poems which are sprinkled throughout this collection. That's not meant to be "hostile", so much as to say that when Halliday lets his voices (and there are many here) be heard for themselves, there are occasions of engaging word-play and wonder in the "glass box[es] that you call a poem".

The three remaining books of this omnibus review are of less interest. Lisa Dart's debut collection, *The Linguistics of Light*, reveals much philosophical pondering at work – words and their defining relationship to the world are consistently mulled over – but it's a simple relationship that's expressed and one that never rises to the occasion of truly dramatising just how central language is to experience. *Crab & Winkle* is the Australian poet Laurie Duggan's 'journal' of his first year living in England. In multi-sectioned poems, Duggan converses with himself about not only his new country (much is set in Kent) but the world of poetry. It's an attempt to pull off the Frank O'Hara feat of recording his day to day with whimsy and wit. Unfortunately, within the sprawl of these poems there's too much of the perfunctory, and all too often the best fragments (where we see a glimmer of what's possible), get lost in the rambling mix.

I'll finish with Giles Goodland's *What the Things Sang*, a sequence of poems each dependent on a type of linguistic or typographical patterning. Most are contrived at the author's own whim, but of reoccurring interest to Goodland is the use of the alphabet to arrange what amounts to many (many) declarative statements which refuse to value one piece of language over another. One poem ends with what seems a punch-line to the twenty-eight random observations that precede it: "arrange these in order of value". These experiments in cataloguing seem lessened by extensive processing.

Anthony Caleshu is the author of *The Siege Of The Body And A Brief Respite*. He is Senior Lecturer in English and Creative Writing at the University of Plymouth.

# The Art Of Poetry

NANCY CAMPBELL

George Szirtes/Ronald King, *The Burning of the Books*, Full Circle Editions, £16, ISBN 9780956186904; Sean O'Brien/Birtley Aris, *Night Train*, Aris Flambard Press, £9.99 ISBN 9781906601089

A popular misconception about illustrated books is that they should be beautiful, or at least humorous. *The Burning of the Books*, issued by veteran book artist Ron King, is neither. Since the 1960s, King's Circle Press has issued elegant and imaginative poetry editions as well as a number of artist's books that contemplate the nature of reading and writing. *The Burning of the Books* combines these interests in a series of poems by George

Szirtes in response to Elias Canetti's novel, *Die Blendung* (1935). This is a violent vision of the disintegration of European society; now known in English as *Auto da Fe*, the title was almost translated, with terrible prescience, as *Holocaust*. The novel's anti-hero, Peter Kien, was modelled on the moral philosopher Immanuel Kant, who, Canetti believed, set fire to his library and burned to death among his books. As Szirtes points out, the subject matter is "close to the bone" of both artist and poet.

Szirtes describes his poems as "a growth around the book": an oblique approach necessitated by copyright issues, but one which serves to acknowledge the pervasive influence all works of art have on each other. A cacophony of half-familiar echoes within these poems confirm that "Culture is a madness everyone inherits." Visual arts are referenced as much as literature. The citizens of Szirtes's cityscape are seen through the eyes of Canetti's artist contemporaries: "the Groszbeggars stirred and shook a leg /And the Dixwounded rattled their small change of limbs" ('Prologue'). The frontispiece is a homage to Picasso's *Guernica*, painted two years after the publication of *Auto da Fe*. The central motif in the painting is a horse, which in King's version is assembled from scraps of lettering, including incunabula, gothic type and graffiti.

Books are unreliable things, which tend to mutate before Szirtes' eyes into people, dreams and dust. They become fierce creatures, such as the jaguars that

> [...] stalk the night streets
> The onion-paper of their eyes flickering and thin,
> The small print of their teeth gathering in the margin,
> The index of their jaws containing everything possible to be
> written [...]   ('Postscriptum')

These animals cannot be subdued by flames, since "the fire is ambiguous / But may be interpreted as a careful close reading". Everything burns but nothing is ever consumed, in the perpetually-burning purgatorial city.

The grotesque caricatures leering from King's collages are snipped from celebrity columns and police files. Disembodied eyes and hands dance across the page, and lips are stretched around soundless shouts. Opposite each collage Szirtes's poems describe a world of mob rule and madhouses. There is conflict in the crowd, in the bed and even on the chessboards in decadent apartments. The streets "are records of blood and boot marks". There are none of the adept *terza rima* or sonnets we might expect from Szirtes here.

Instead "a series of narrative cries and thrusts" creates a feeling of chaos. Yet his use of language to interrogate language remains as uncomfortably elegant as a Leni Riefenstahl film. Words are both dangerous and endangered things:

> To eat books is to have a stomach full of corners,
> Because the word is angular and has sharp edges
> that cut you: consonants, sibilants, gutturals,
> No sound is free from danger, everything harms you.
>
> ('Consuming passion')

This brilliant poem describes a debate between a scholar and a dwarf on whether the flesh or the mind is superior. "It is ourselves / Not the books we eat" that count, according to the dwarf. But the scholar believes "A thin man survives on a colophon". There is a wealth of aphorisms in these poems, but like a dictator's rhetoric, each needs to be picked apart.

Nothing is what it seems in *Night Train*, Sean O'Brien's new homage to the railway. At first glance the slim volume might be a sketchbook, discarded on a station platform or discovered amidst fireweed on a railway siding. Handwritten poems, crossings out, energetic line drawings, all suggest a work in progress. But telltale pencil lines, not quite erased from the page, carefully guide the ink calligraphy like iron rails. It becomes evident that this is a fine copy. The drawings, conducted with the same pen, perfectly balance the timbre of the verse.

If water pervaded *The Drowned Book*, the element of *Night Train* is darkness. There's an occasional mention of dusk, but most of these poems happen by night, or undercover of "New arches, further demarcations of / The darkness in the ramifying dark" ('Closed'). The tunnel is a metaphor for all oblivion, and the traveller fears, "As if each darkness were the last of all" ('Inheritance'). In these sacred spaces, O'Brien feels "It would be sacrilege to put a word / Into that open silent mouth, that waits / And does not wait, while nothing comes." ('Bridge')

The artist Birtley Aris also works with stained glass, and an awareness of how light falls into a room, or onto a page, is evident in the architecture of *Night Train*. Panels of white space or of print create dynamic spreads. Drawings tumble out of their frames. This is a book of filmic perspectives. Sketches pan across a landscape in which telegraph wires disappear into the distance. A train shoots across a night landscape like a glow-worm. Close-ups zoom into seemingly innocuous shrubbery, dimly-lit Pullman compartments and stormy, cross-hatched skies. It's a homage, not only to the train, but also for an era of English noir when fictional detectives solved every crime and the Night Mail ran on time.

It is so hard to interpret these dark images – as tricky as squinting through a keyhole – that the viewer may feel a sense of transgression. The poems also suggest voyeurism, as in the closed café where we see

> Change counted out in half-pennies, received
> With patience and a joke that no one but
> The waitress and her pink-necked soldier hear.   ('Closed')

Currency, and cast,  set this book in the same time-frame as Canetti, but here scenes are observed with affection rather than horror.

Found poems, including railway ephemera and advertising hoardings ('ENJOY THE FRESH AIR AND BEE  SANDWICHES'), scatter the book. Messages on picture postcards interweave the poems, growing increasingly frantic as they appear to go unread by the narrator's object of desire: "Let me know I will wait at the gates as before". O'Brien intersperses station announcements with fragments from the *Georgics*: "Lost song of the Apparatus / A pastorail" [*sic*]. The poem reflects the experience of reading whilst travelling, but also implies an affinity between the lost agricultural way of life lamented by Virgil and nostalgia for "the whole / Implied immensity of England" which remains just beyond reach ('Reasonable Men'). Thoreau, watching the railroad encroach on his beloved Walden, declared, "We have constructed a fate, an *Atropos*, that never turns aside." Of course, we save our strongest nostalgia for fantasy:

> You had to be there, you suppose. You never were.
> It's in the way you tell 'em, in the fact
> You know so well what you could never find.   ('Closed')

O'Brien clearly loves the train as a metaphor as much as he cherishes its mechanics.  The last postcard on the flyleaf of *Night Train* finds the narrator still waiting "to catch the dawn train".

Nancy Campbell is an artists' book maker and has written widely on the form. In 2010 she will be writer-in-residence at Upernavik Museum, Greenland.

# THE INTERN REVIEW

# From Llagerrub To Belgrade

JAKE ELLIOTT

Meirion Jordan, *Moonrise*, Seren Books, £7.99 ISBN 9781854114815;
Chris McCabe, *Zeppelins*, Salt Publishing, £12.99 ISBN 9781844714384;
Matthew Welton, *We needed coffee but...*, Carcanet,
£9.95 ISBN 9781857770028;
James Sutherland-Smith, *Popeye in Belgrade*, Carcanet,
£9.95 ISBN 9781857549690;
Chris McCully, *Polder*, Carcanet, £9.95 ISBN 9781847770172

M oonrise, the debut collection from Welsh poet Meirion Jordan, explores a range of differing topics with evident curiosity. I can't help but feel that the poems themselves are born of an organic force, shaped and formed primarily by the fertility of their own content. Jordan often favours the phrase unbroken over stanzas and as such his poetry takes on characteristics of the smoothed pebbles in 'Calculus': "shadows meeting them as they kiss / the meniscus over and over with the lightness / of an eclipse."

The blurb suggests that Jordan's poetry admixes *Under Milk Wood* and a J. G. Ballard novel, and it is in this stylistic partnership that problems begin to arise. Jordan's imagery often seems to trigger some dormant familiarity, or perhaps an active familiarity, bordering on cliché. In 'Sky Writing', Jordan's enigmatic sky-gazer feels too sweet in the mouth, as the speaker "pours the tea" and fears she may fly away. Lexical inclusions such as "Saturn Five", "ionosphere" and "errata of a jet stream" seem to show the poet adopting novelty in an attempt to rescue the poem from sentimentality. This forced synthesis sometimes damages his writing. Portraits, such as 'Girl on a Motorbike in India', 'A Horse in the Dark' and 'Moonrise' are Jordan's best work. The first of these seems so natural that it could have been scrawled on the back of a fondled sepia photograph. Moments of naturaliness are also suggested at other points in the collection before the splinters of contrivance disrupt his pastoral visions.

Merion Jordan the mathematician poet appears to believe that poetry's relationship with otherworldliness lies in allusions to Philip K Dick and Yuri Gagarin. He doesn't seem to allow space for the possibility of a more profound connection than this.

Chris McCabe, on the other hand, seems able casually to render huge political topics into small dense lines pregnant with meaning and humour. His is a talent for packaging. In his latest collection, *Zeppelins*, McCabe squeezes his subject matter for its essence, which he delivers in precise colloquial packets of poetry.

Pete Doherty, BNP rallies, emotive confessionals, and poems on marriage appear side by side and yet do not rupture the sense of a complete whole. Lines such as, "at the hub of news content / page 110 said / Blasts Won't Shake UK Economy" are paradigmatic of McCabe's wit and poignancy. His lines after Tom Leonard are lucid, acute and will appeal to poet and musician alike.

Reading J.K.Huysmans's *A Rebours* alongside Matthew Welton's latest collection *We Needed Coffee But...* has been an illuminating experience. Huysmans's is an aesthetic exploration of the *mal du siècle*: which triumphs where Welton's poetry fails. Huysmans's treatment of sensual isolation and immersion is an art form in itself, the ekphrastic mélange of nature and artifice is hypnotic and profound. It is impossible to say this of Welton's poetry, though its intentions are similar.

Welton's poems are concerned with ambiguous notions of character and lexical nomenclature: modern abstraction. The poet challenges his reader to penetrate the dense repetitive nature of his poetry in order to root out epistemological questions. As a result one is often faced with a jarring thematic confrontation of formal and semantic artifice and realism, and ultimately a prolonged, tiring search. Artifice is inherent in Welton's poetry. Yet it's a theme by which the poet seems daunted. He retreats into solipsistic ambiguity, where a braver poet would have abandoned the sinking ship of post-modernism. This dedication to a leaky vessel of contradictory ideals damages the book. The poet deftly dabbles with silences in his prose poem 'Virtual Airport' – "The public address plays a mumbling kind of music. The corridor / becomes less crowded. A group of girls goes by" – yet these flourishes are stifled by an obsession with technique.

The section 'Six Poems by Themselves', in which six poetic structures are illustrated by literal *lines* across a page, is a low point. However, it is an astonishingly honest metaphor for this collection. Welton seems to have become intimidated by his own aim; he struggles with the idea of innovation, tangling notions in metaphor and simile, before regressing and submitting to the vacancy of pure structures. In 'Coda', he writes, "More push-pull lush-lull hush-mush-mull / Grab your flab, grab your drib-drab crab-slab": with arched eyebrow asking the reader to fill his denotative vacancy with any notion that will justify the poem's existence. Contrast this with Huysmans's treatment of vacancy, restricted pleasures and boundless desire, artifice and the reinterpretation of nature.

James Sutherland-Smith's glancing encounters with Balkan culture inform *Popeye in Belgrade*, his second collection. Sutherland-Smith worked for the British Council with the Peacekeeping Forces in the white city for four years. Despite this, the collection is surprisingly facile. Carcanet tell us "He writes, not as an observer, but from within cultures [...]" Unfortunately this is simply not true. The poet writes accounts of Serbia that could appear on postcards; pretty or sometimes harrowing, but predictable, sterile and safe:

> Outside the church we wrap our natures
> Against the cold wind and the snow.

Having recently travelled to Belgrade myself, I was struck by Sutherland-Smith's reluctance to turn his eye to anything but the most predictable facets of the city, "War compels new, painful starts though I'm old here / Among proud young Serbs, jet-haired, hand in hand." The poet's painfully pedestrian description of local Serbs as "jet-haired" is obvious and disappointing. As a writer "within cultures" the poet should understand the synchronous nature of Belgrade's desire to evolve and the raw presence of its past. Encountering a village welcome from a small community delighted to embrace outsiders into their patchwork culture with plate after plate of red meat (comatose grandmothers in the corner) made me particularly aware of the hands-off character of Sutherland-Smith's approach.

However, he is capable of occasional honesty. 'In a Slovak Garden' illustrates the dichotomy of the poet's viewpoint:

> 'Don't break the earth. Don't break the earth.'

> I understand. I understand,
> But I try to tell them all
> That we do not have hard frosts
> In England, that my digging
> Is from habits of my youth.

Sutherland-Smith's "habits of youth" must have been safety and caricatures. He does not "understand." This is a poetry of distance in the face of proximity.

A very different European context is provided by Chris McCully's *Polder*. His fifth collection, it is based around the poet's recovery from alcoholism, his fiftieth year and his life in Holland. Although the collection features four chapters it is the first, 'Dust', in which McCully fully realises his strategy and ability. The remainder of this collection concerns itself with McCully's musings on belonging, journeying and separation.

'Dust' is a prose poem which exhibits the poet's considerable gifts for evoking mood and for self-inspection. Its thematic crescendo is all the more effective for the poetic rhythms entailed. McCully punches into his first staves *staccato*: "I have looked into dust." The poem then takes a series of sluggish, almost false 'steps' of realisation, epitomised in the poet's use of Latin declension, "Amo, amas, amat; mensa, mensa, mensam". However, 'Dust' transcends these restrictive linguistic, metaphorical, and ideological steps. Its crescendo is preceded by a downwards spiral of conditional imperatives – "Be what I want, not what you need" – before his ideas begin to gather speed and altitude. The penultimate section is a cathartic triumph. The poet reaches his lowest point mentally, yet poetically he soars:

> Out came the grey smear of a dawn over city skylines, and
> a nest of spiders. Out came the blood of a summer
> afternoon.

Jake Elliott is the current intern at *Poetry Review*. He read English at UCW Swansesa and has researched into Romanticism.

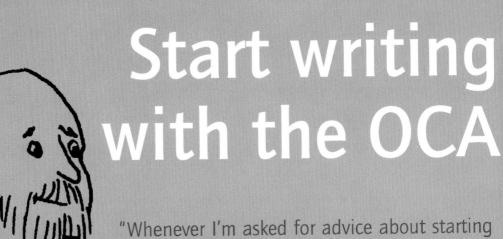

# ALBUM

envelope
full
winter
  – *Uriankhai*

# Merging Cultures:
# A Month In Mongolia

RUTH O'CALLAGHAN

Ulaanbaatar glowers but early morning sun alleviates Soviet tower-block-grey as my driver – thoughtfully provided by the Writers' Union – skims through the heaving mesh of traffic towards my apartment, also thoughtfully provided. Poets are revered in Mongolia but there appears to be little or no state funding for the art. Public finance, such as it is, is directed towards branches of engineering and technology to enable development of the country's infrastructure.

Landlocked between Russia and China, both powers anxious to exploit her rich deposits of gold, silver, copper and coal, Mongolia is a country in a state of flux. Approximately 45% of the population, attracted away from the harsh life of the steppe by the promise of cars, mobile phones, hot water and flushing toilets, have now migrated to the capital: bringing problems with housing, social welfare, water and electricity supplies.

Lack of electricity prevented my reading in the Museum of Fine Arts – power wasn't available in that part of town that day. Another gallery, commandeered at a moment's notice, welcomed the guests, including the Ambassador of the United States, press, radio, Mongolia's eminent poets and Honoured Persons, without hesitation. This is Mongolia – constantly creating solutions from chaos.

Mongolian poetry is proudly embedded in nationalism and traditions surrounding Chinggis Khan, as well as the beauty of their land, family and community life. As such it accurately reflects everyday society. U.B. has the Chinggis Khan Irish Pub; on the steppe a bill board demands *Investors wanted* for the Chinggis Khan Country Club; whilst in an isolated *gyr* in the Gobi strangers are offered hospitality by a family who fiercely protest that their bloodline, from Chinggis, must remain pure.

Chinggis promoted religious tolerance: and Bhuddism, despite over fifty years of oppression, remains a vital force, with religion, poetry and politics seemingly intertwined. The nineteenth century monk-poet Danzanravjaa – who still influences today's poets such as G.A. Ayurzana – was poisoned by the Qing dynasty in 1856, whilst a similar fate befell Dashbalbar in 1999 after he exposed corrupt politicians. The nationalistic poems 'My Native Land' and 'Star' by Dashdorjiin, regarded as the founder of Mongolian literature, find an echo in Dulmaa Shagdar's 'I Love My Soil', Suglegmaa Khurgaa's 'The Essence' and Munkhtsegtseg Gompildoo's 'Don't Betray My Song'.

Yet desire for progress is evident. The poet Ulziitugs Luvsandorjiin articulates this dichotomy and the self-doubt it entails: "Dashdorjiin is my favourite poet. He is great lyricist. 'Native Land' reminds me of a photo collage of beautiful nature, but I like more non-realistic creations. Chinggis Khan is our national pride, he had greatest spiritual power. All world knows that we have great history. But, I think, we have not lived by only great past to fight with today's many problems; 'I believe in yesterday' but in my mind his influence on today's Mongolia is zero. Maybe, I'm not right."

One man who epitomises Mongolia on the cusp of change is Dr. Mend-Oyoo, President of the Academy of Poetry and Culture, a quietly-spoken man of enormous influence, indeed power. Constantly flying around the world, or being in touch via his mobile with poets from many different cultures as he drives through traffic-fumed streets, he nevertheless writes poetry and prose infused with yearning for "A mirage on the blue steppe, like a heavenly city" ('Paradise and Swallows'), the nomadic life that was his boyhood, and reverence for his ancestors.

Mend-Oyoo's office is a United Nations of poets, writers, academics and translators but every 'arm' of literature – the Union of Mongolian Writers and the Arts Council of Mongolia – is thrusting forward towards the West. Under the Soviets in fact, Uriankhai's three word poem:

> envelope
> full
> winter

was denounced as the devil's poem – despite the devil's also being banned. Since the democratic revolution, many new poets have emerged. Certainly it is doubtful whether Enkhboldbaatar's poem 'A Set (Absolute Values)', with its surrealistically random world, would have ever been published previously.

> point (not a new start),
> one (this is the real start),
> comma (links a
> numerical sequence),
> fifty six (not an age, not an order, not
> anything),

Over lunch, Enkhboldbaatar spoke of founding the U.B. Boys – a group of young men who perform their poetry – and how he continually pushes against the boundaries of form and structure. As a playwright and screenwriter he too is anxious for recognition in the West, but was rather disconcerted when I mentioned that many women poets in England feel that the poetry scene here is male dominated. (Perhaps especially so as he was at that moment playing me a CD of female poets.) Apparently gender has never been an issue and Enkhboldbaatar endorses Ulziitugs's claim that "Nomads' wives had more right to control of her family's money. This tradition is still alive in our poetry. I never felt that I'm second sex between literary men." (Note the interesting implication of a money-poetry equation.)

Since the rise of English in schools – the language was previously condemned as a tool of ideological enemies – many poets are euphoric about the times in which they live. Some have 'switched allegiance' from Russian to Western writers. Indeed, wherever I went I was quizzed on *Beowulf*, Chaucer, Dickens, Dickinson, Stevens, whilst the poet D. Sukhbaatar proudly recited from his translation of the whole of Shakespeare's sonnets into Mongolian. (It is rumoured that he's about to begin on the Tragedies.)

However, the lessening of Soviet domination also brought about the demise of an efficient book distribution system. Poets now pay for publication, deliver their own books to the shops, which extract a hefty commission, and each month collect the pittance that remains. Lack of state involvement – money – in this process is bemoaned but seen as the price for lack of state censorship.

Mongolians dream of a politician who has the stature of a Chinggis. Perhaps, from their idealised Western model of publisher/distributor, an entrepreneur will emerge to create such an empire for poetry.

# SOME CONTRIBUTORS

**Dannie Abse**'s new novel, *Two for Joy*, is forthcoming from Hutchinson in February. **Linda Maria Baros** has two books of poetry in Romanian and two in French. *La maison en lames de rasoir* (2006), was awarded the Prix Apollinaire in 2007. **Peter Blegvad** is an iconoclast, musician, artist and faculty member of the Warwick Writing Programme. **Wendy Cope**'s most recent publication is *Two Cures for Love: selected poems 1979-2006*. **Fred D'Aguiar**'s sixth collection, *Continental Shelf* (Carcanet, 2009) is a PBS Choice. **Gerald Dawe**'s collections include *Points West* (2008). He is a fellow of Trinity College Dublin. **John F. Deane**'s most recent collection is *A Little Book of Hours* (Carcanet, 2008), published in Italian as *Piccolo Libro delle Ore* (Kolibris, 2009). **Carol Ann Duffy** is the Poet Laureate. **Maureen Duffy** is a distinguished poet and novelist whose latest collection is *Family Values* (2008). **Katherine Gallagher**'s *Carnival Edge: New & Selected Poems* is due from Arc in March 2010. **Linda Gregerson**'s most recent book of poetry, *Magnetic North* (Houghton Mifflin, 2007) was a finalist for the National Book Award. **David Harsent**'s *Selected Poems* was shortlisted for the Griffin International Poetry prize. *The Minotaur* and *The Corridor* opened recently at ROH and the Aldeburgh Festival. **Rita Ann Higgins** is a well-known Irish poet. **Lyubomir Levchev** is a leading Bulgarian poet. **Tim Liardet**'s *The Storm House* is due from Carcanet in 2011. **Sean O'Brien**'s *The Drowned Book* (2007) won the Forward and T.S. Eliot prizes. His novel *Afterlife* appeared in summer 2009. **Ruth O'Callaghan** has been translated into German, Italian, Hungarian, Romanian and Mongolian and was awarded an Arts Council grant to visit Mongolia. **Jeri Onitskansky** is a Jungian analyst who lives and works in High Barnet. **Sigitas Parulskis** is a Lithuanian novelist and poet whose work features in *PR*'s supplement to 98:1. **Mario Petrucci** won the Cinequest award for his poetry film, *Half Life: a Journey to Chernobyl*. *i tulips* (Enitharmon) is due in March. **Jacob Polley**'s second collection was *Little Gods*. **J.S. Randall** spent the last couple of years in America where a number of his poems have appeared in magazines. **Stephen Raw** is a lettering artist who has worked on a number of collaborations with Carol Ann Duffy. **Robin Robertson**'s *The Wrecking Light* will be published in February. **Carol Rumens**'s latest collection is *Blind Spots* (Seren, 2007). **Tracy Ryan** is an Australian novelist and poet, whose latest books are *Scar Revision* and *Sweet* (both 2008). **Tomaž Šalamun** is the leading Slovenian poet, extensively published in the US, this year awarded the Golden Wreath of Struga. **Peter Sansom**'s pamphlet, *The Night is Young* is just out from *The Rialto*, and *Selected Poems* will appear from Carcanet in autumn 2010. **Adam J. Sorkin**'s translation of Marin Sorescu (with Lidia Vianu, Bloodaxe,) won the 2005 Corneliu M. Popescu Prize. **Anne Stevenson**'s *Collected Poems 1955–2005* (Bloodaxe) won several major prizes. *Stone Milk* appeared in 2008. **Matthew Sweeney**'s revised *Collected Poems* will appear from Salt in 2010. **George Volceanov** has won honors from the Writers' Association of Bucharest, the British Council, the Romanian Writers' Museum, and the Romanian Writers' Union. **Sam Willetts**'s first collection is forthcoming from Cape in April.